SPYWARE

SPYWARE

JOHN S. YANG
EDITOR

Novinka Books
New York

Copyright © 2005 by Novinka Books
An imprint of Nova Science Publishers, Inc.

All rights reserved. No part of this book may be reproduced, stored in a retrieval system or transmitted in any form or by any means: electronic, electrostatic, magnetic, tape, mechanical photocopying, recording or otherwise without the written permission of the Publisher.

For permission to use material from this book please contact us:
Telephone 631-231-7269; Fax 631-231-8175
Web Site: http://www.novapublishers.com

NOTICE TO THE READER

The Publisher has taken reasonable care in the preparation of this book, but makes no expressed or implied warranty of any kind and assumes no responsibility for any errors or omissions. No liability is assumed for incidental or consequential damages in connection with or arising out of information contained in this book. The Publisher shall not be liable for any special, consequential, or exemplary damages resulting, in whole or in part, from the readers' use of, or reliance upon, this material.

This publication is designed to provide accurate and authoritative information with regard to the subject matter covered herein. It is sold with the clear understanding that the Publisher is not engaged in rendering legal or any other professional services. If legal or any other expert assistance is required, the services of a competent person should be sought. FROM A DECLARATION OF PARTICIPANTS JOINTLY ADOPTED BY A COMMITTEE OF THE AMERICAN BAR ASSOCIATION AND A COMMITTEE OF PUBLISHERS.

Library of Congress Cataloging-in-Publication Data:
Available Upon Request

ISBN: 1-59454-648-7

Published by Nova Science Publishers, Inc. ✦ *New York*

CONTENTS

Preface		vii
Chapter 1	Spyware: Background and Policy Issues for Congress *Marcia S. Smith*	1
Chapter 2	Monitoring Software on Your PC: Spyware, Adware, and Other Software *Staff Report*	29

PREFACE

The term "spyware" is not well defined. Generally it is used to refer to any software that is downloaded onto a person's computer without their knowledge. Spyware may collect information about a computer user's activities and transmit that information to someone else. It may change computer settings, or cause "pop-up" advertisements to appear (in that context, it is called "adware"). Spyware may redirect a Web browser to a site different from what the user intended to visit, or change the user's home page. A type of spyware called "keylogging" software records individual keystrokes, even if the author modifies or deletes what was written, or if the characters do not appear on the monitor. Thus, passwords, credit card numbers, and other personally identifiable information may be captured and relayed to unauthorized recipients. Some of these software programs have legitimate applications the computer user wants. They obtain the moniker "spyware" when they are installed surreptitiously, or perform additional functions of which the user is unaware. Users typically do not realize that spyware is on their computer. They may have unknowingly downloaded it from the Internet by clicking within a website, or it might have been included in an attachment to an electronic mail message (e-mail) or embedded in other software. According to a survey and tests conducted by America Online and the National Cyber Security Alliance, 80% of computers in the test group were infected by spyware or adware, and 89% of the users of those computers were unaware of it. The Federal Trade Commission (FTC) issued a consumer alert on spyware in October 2004. It provided a list of warning signs that might indicate that a computer is infected with spyware, and advice on what to do if it is.This new book helps shed light on this insidious nightmare created by members of the human race to wreck havoc on the remainder.

Chapter 1

SPYWARE: BACKGROUND AND POLICY ISSUES FOR CONGRESS[*]

Marcia S. Smith

ABSTRACT

The term "spyware" is not well defined. Generally it is used to refer to any software that is downloaded onto a person's computer without their knowledge. Spyware may collect information about a computer user's activities and transmit that information to someone else. It may change computer settings, or cause "pop-up" advertisements to appear (in that context, it is called "adware"). Spyware may redirect a Web browser to a site different from what the user intended to visit, or change the user's home page. A type of spyware called "keylogging" software records individual keystrokes, even if the author modifies or deletes what was written, or if the characters do not appear on the monitor. Thus, passwords, credit card numbers, and other personally identifiable information may be captured and relayed to unauthorized recipients.

Some of these software programs have legitimate applications the computer user wants. They obtain the moniker "spyware" when they are installed surreptitiously, or perform additional functions of which the user is unaware. Users typically do not realize that spyware is on their computer. They may have unknowingly downloaded it from the Internet by clicking within a website, or it might have been included in an attachment to an electronic mail message (e-mail) or embedded in other software. According

---

[*] Excerpted from CRS Report RL32706 dated April 4, 2005.

to a survey and tests conducted by America Online and the National Cyber Security Alliance, 80% of computers in the test group were infected by spyware or adware, and 89% of the users of those computers were unaware of it. The Federal Trade Commission (FTC) issued a consumer alert on spyware in October 2004. It provided a list of warning signs that might indicate that a computer is infected with spyware, and advice on what to do if it is.

Utah and California have passed spyware laws, but there is no specific federal law regarding spyware. The 109th Congress is considering H.R. 29, H.R. 744, and S. 687. The two House bills are similar to bills that passed the House in 2004. H.R. 29 was ordered reported from the House Energy and Commerce Committee on March 9, 2005.

A central point of the debate is whether new laws are needed, or if industry selfregulation, coupled with enforcement actions under existing laws such as the Federal Trade Commission Act, is sufficient. The lack of a precise definition for spyware is cited as a fundamental problem in attempting to write new laws. FTC representatives and others caution that new legislation could have unintended consequences, barring current or future technologies that might, in fact, have beneficial uses. They further insist that, if legal action is necessary, existing laws provide sufficient authority. Consumer concern about control of their computers being taken over by spyware, and resulting impacts on their privacy, leads others to conclude that legislative action is needed.

BACKGROUND

Congress is debating whether to enact new legislation to deal with the growing problem of "spyware." Spyware is not well defined, but generally includes software emplaced on a computer without the user's knowledge that takes control of the computer away from the user, such as by redirecting the computer to unintended websites, causing advertisements to appear, or collecting information and transmitting it to another person. The lack of a firm definition of the term adds to the complexities of drafting new laws.

The Federal Trade Commission (FTC) and others argue that industry selfregulation, and enforcement of existing laws, are sufficient. They worry that further legislation could have unintended consequences that, for example, limit the development of new technologies that could have beneficial uses. The 108th Congress debated spyware legislation, and two bills passed the House, but neither cleared Congress. Debate has resumed in the 109th Congress. Pending legislation is discussed later in this report.

What is Spyware?

The term "spyware" is not well defined. Jerry Berman, President of the Center for Democracy and Technology (CDT), explained in testimony to the Subcommittee on Communications of the Senate Commerce, Science, and Transportation Committee in March 2004 that "The term has been applied to software ranging from 'keystroke loggers' that capture every key typed on a particular computer; to advertising applications that track users' web browsing; to programs that hijack users' system settings." [1] He noted that what these various types of software programs "have in common is a lack of transparency and an absence of respect for users' ability to control their own computers and Internet connections."

Software programs that include spyware may be sold or available for free ("freeware"). They may be on a disk or other media, downloaded from the Internet, or downloaded when opening an attachment to an electronic mail (e-mail) message. Typically, users have no knowledge that spyware is on their computers. Because the spyware is resident on the computer's hard drive, it can generate pop-up ads, for example, even when the computer is not connected to the Internet.

One example of spyware is software products that include, as part of the software itself, a method by which information is collected about the use of the computer on which the software is installed, such as Web browsing habits. Some of these products may collect personally identifiable information (PII). When the computer is connected to the Internet, the software periodically relays the information back to another party, such as the software manufacturer or a marketing company. Another oft-cited example of spyware is "**adware**," which may cause advertisements to suddenly appear on the user's monitor — called "pop-up" ads. In some cases, the adware uses information that the software obtained by tracking a user's Web browsing habits to determine shopping preferences, for example.

As Mr. Berman explained, spyware also can refer to "keylogging" software that records a person's keystrokes. All typed information thus can be obtained by another party, even if the author modifies or deletes what was written, or if the characters do not appear on the monitor (such as when entering a password). Commercial key logging software has been available for some time. [2] In the context of the spyware debate, the concern is that such software can record credit card numbers and other personally identifiable information that consumers type when using Internet-based shopping and financial services, and transmit that information to someone else. Thus it could contribute to identity theft. [3]

As discussed below, the lack of a precise definition for spyware is often cited by opponents of legislation as a reason not to legislate. They argue that without a definition, legislation could have unintended consequences, banning current or future technologies and activities that, in fact, could be beneficial. Some of these software applications, including adware and keylogging software, have legitimate uses. The question is whether the user has given consent for it to be installed.

Prevalence of Spyware

In October 2004, America Online (AOL) and the National Cyber Security Alliance (NCSA) [4] released the results of a survey of 329 dial-up and broadband computer users regarding online threats, including spyware. [5] According to the study:

- 80% of the computers they tested were infected with spyware or adware, and 89% of the users of those computers were unaware of it;
- the average infected computer had 93 spyware/adware components on it, and the most found on a single computer was 1,059; and
- most users do not recognize the symptoms of spyware — 63% of users with a pop-up blocker said they got pop-up ads anyway, 43% of users said their home page had been changed without their permission, and 40% said their search results are being redirected or changed.

Separately, Webroot Software, a provider of privacy and protection software, released the results of a survey of 287 corporate information technology managers on October 27, 2004. That survey concluded that although more than 70% of corporations expressed increased concern about spyware, less than 10% had implemented commercially available anti-spyware software. [6]

A representative of Dell Inc. told the *Washington Post* that between August 2003 and October 2004, customer support calls related to spyware rose from about 2% to 10-15%. [7]

FTC Advice to Consumers

The FTC issued a consumer alert about spyware in October 2004 offering a list of warning signs that might indicate that a computer is infected with spyware. [8] The FTC alert listed the following clues:

- a barrage of pop-up ads;
- a hijacked browser — that is, a browser that takes you to sites other than those you type into the address box;
- a sudden or repeated change in your computer's Internet home page;
- new and unexpected toolbars;
- new and unexpected icons on the system tray at the bottom of your computer screen;
- keys that don't work (for example, the "Tab" key that might not work when you try to move to the next field in a Web form);
- random error messages; and
- sluggish or downright slow performance when opening programs or saving files.

The FTC alert also offered preventive actions consumers can take:

- update your operating system and Web browser software;
- download free software only from sites you know and trust;
- don't install any software without knowing exactly what it is;
- minimize "drive-by" downloads by ensuring that your browser's security setting is high enough to detect unauthorized downloads;
- don't click on any links within pop-up windows;
- don't click on links in spam that claim to offer anti-spyware software; and
- install a personal firewall to stop uninvited users from accessing your computer.

Finally, the FTC alert advised consumers who think their computers are infected to get an anti-spyware program from a vendor they know and trust; set it to scan on a regular basis, at startup and at least once a week; and delete any software programs detected by the anti-spyware program that the consumer does not want.

Reviews of some of the commercially available anti-spyware programs are available in magazines such as PC World and Consumer Reports. [9]

Other FTC Activities

The FTC held a workshop on spyware on April 19, 2004. [10] The director of FTC's Bureau of Consumer Protection, Howard Beales, summarized the workshop at a hearing before the Subcommittee on Telecommunications and the Internet of the House Energy and Commerce Committee 10 days later. He listed a number of ways in which spyware can harm consumers and businesses.

.... It seems clear from the workshop's discussions spyware may harvest personally identifiable information from consumers through monitoring computer use without consent. It also may facilitate identity theft by surreptitiously planting a keystroke logger on a user's computer.

Spyware may create security risks if it exposes communications channels to hackers. It also may effect [sic] the operation of personal computers, causing crashes, browser hijacking, homepage resetting and the like. These harms are problems in themselves and could lead to a loss in consumer confidence in the Internet as a medium of communication and commerce.

Second, many of the panelists discussed how spyware may cause problems for businesses, too. Companies may incur costs as they seek to block and remove spyware from computers of their employees or their customers. Employees will also be less productive if spyware causes their computers to crash or if they're distracted...by a barrage of pop-up ads. Spyware that captures the keystrokes of employees could be used to obtain trade secrets and confidential information from businesses. [11]

Mr. Beale also listed a number of ways in which the computer industry is attempting to help consumers and businesses cope with the spyware problem, for example through development of anti-spyware programs.

An FTC staff report on the results of the workshop was published in March 2005. [12] The report concluded that addressing the spyware problem will require a coordinated and sustained effort on the part of the private sector and government.

The FTC also has taken legal action to stop spyware practices. The Commission filed its first spyware case in October 2004 in response to a complaint filed by the Center for Democracy and Technology (CDT). In an October 12, 2004 press release, [13] the FTC explained that it was charging Sanford Wallace and two companies with which he is associated,

Smartbot.Net and Seismic Entertainment Productions. Inc., with unfair and deceptive practices for using a variety of techniques to direct consumers to their websites where spyware was downloaded onto their computer without notice or consent. The FTC asserts that the spyware created serious problems on those computers, and the defendants thereupon offered to sell the consumers software for $30 to fix the problems. The FTC asked the U.S. District Court, District of New Hampshire, "to issue an order preventing the defendants from disseminating spyware and giving up their ill-gotten gains." [14] Mr. Wallace denied wrongdoing. [15] U.S. District Judge Joseph DiClerico issued a temporary restraining order against the defendants on October 21, 2004. [16]

State Laws

In March 2004, Utah became the first state to pass spyware legislation. California followed in September. In testimony to the House Energy and Commerce Committee's Subcommittee on Telecommunications and the Internet in April 2004, FTC Commissioner Mozelle Thompson not only called on Congress to give industry an opportunity to self-regulate, but also asked states to "be cautious" about passing such legislation because "a patchwork of differing and inconsistent state approaches might be confusing to industry and consumers alike." [17]

Utah

On March 23, 2004, the Governor of Utah, Olene Walker, signed the first state anti-spyware law, which became effective on May 3, 2004. [18] The definition of spyware in that law includes certain pop-up ads. It prohibits, for example, some popup ads that partially or wholly cover or obscure paid advertising or other content on a website in a way that interferes with a user's ability to view the website. A media report stated that passage of the law was "driven by a Utah company in a legal fight with a pop-up company." [19] The Utah law also defines spyware, inter alia, as software installed on a computer without the user's consent and that cannot be easily disabled and removed. Several high-tech companies reportedly argued that the law could have unintended consequences, for example, prohibiting parents from installing software to block access by their children to certain Websites because the software monitors Web activities, may have been installed without the child's consent, and the child may not be able to uninstall it easily. [20]

WhenU, an adware company, filed suit against the Utah law on constitutional grounds. [21] (WhenU's President and CEO, Avi Naider, testified to the Senate Commerce Committee's Subcommittee on Communications about spyware in March 2004. See **Industry Positions**, below.) The Third Judicial District Court in Salt Lake City, Utah granted a preliminary injunction on June 22, 2004, preventing the law from taking effect. [22]

California

California Governor Arnold Schwarzenegger signed a spyware bill into law on September 28, 2004, [23] which went into effect on January 1, 2005. Inter alia, the law prohibits a person or entity other than the authorized used of a computer — with actual knowledge, conscious avoidance of actual knowledge, or willfully — to cause software to be downloaded onto a computer and using it to take control of the computer, as specified; modify certain settings; collect PII; prevent reasonable efforts to block the installation of or disable the software; intentionally misrepresent that the software will not be installed or will be disabled; or through intentionally deceptive means, remove, disable, or render inoperative certain other software programs on the computer (security, antispyware, or antivirus). Critics argue that the law does not address many spyware-type practices, such as adware. [24]

ISSUES FOR CONGRESS

The 109th Congress has resumed debate on the spyware issue. Two bills are pending in the House: H.R. 29 (Bono) and H.R. 744 (Goodlatte). One has been introduced in the Senate : S. 687 (Burns). Those bills are summarized later in this report. In the 108th Congress, the House passed two spyware bills, and a bill was reported from committee in the Senate. They are summarized in the Appendix.

Debate Over the Need for Federal Spyware Legislation

The main issue for Congress is whether to enact new legislation specifically addressing spyware, or to rely on industry self-regulation and enforcement actions by the FTC and the Department of Justice under existing law.

Advocates of legislation want specific laws to stop spyware. For example, they want software providers to be required to obtain the consent of an authorized user of a computer ("opt-in") before any software is downloaded onto that computer. Skeptics contend that spyware is difficult to define and consequently legislation could have unintended consequences, and that legislation is likely to be ineffective. One argument is that the "bad actors" are not likely to obey any opt-in requirement, but are difficult to locate and prosecute. Also, some are overseas and not subject to U.S. law. Other arguments are that one member of a household (a child, for example) might unwittingly opt-in to spyware that others in the family would know to decline, or that users might not read through a lengthy licensing agreement to ascertain precisely what they are accepting.

In many ways, the debate over how to cope with spyware parallels the controversy that led to unsolicited commercial electronic mail ("spam") legislation. [25] Whether to enact a new law, or rely on enforcement of existing law and industry selfregulation, were the cornerstones of that debate as well. Congress chose to pass the CAN-SPAM Act (P.L. 108-187). Questions remain about that law's effectiveness. MX Logic, a provider of "email defense solutions,"reported that, in November 2004, the percentage of unsolicited commercial e-mails that were compliant with the law was only 6% (up from 4% the previous month). [26] The report that the vast majority of commercial e-mails are not complying with the law fuels the argument that spyware legislation similarly cannot stop the threat. In the case of spam, FTC officials emphasized that consumers should not expect any legislation to solve the spam problem — that consumer education and technological advancements also are needed. The same likely is true for spyware, too.

FTC's Position

The FTC has not taken a formal position on the spyware issue, but two commissioners have stated that they do not support new legislation at this time. Commissioner Orson Swindle reportedly told a March 4, 2005 technology forum sponsored by Citizens Against Government Waste that the government should "walk slowly" on such issues, noting that participants in the spyware debate cannot even agree on a definition of the term. [27] He reportedly called for Congress to focus on expanding enforcement of existing laws against bad actors, rather than further regulation of software makers.

At a November 5, 2004 luncheon sponsored by the Cato Institute, [28] Mr. Swindle expressed similar views, and also called on industry to develop effective approaches to counteract spyware — through self-regulation, adopting standards, consumer education, business education, assisting the government in finding the people doing the harm, and monitoring their own advertising (and whom they hire to do advertising on their behalf). He added that if industry did not solve the problem, by necessity the government would need to act. At a hearing before the House Energy and Commerce Committee's Telecommunications and the Internet subcommittee on April 29, 2004, Commissioner Mozelle Thompson argued that industry should be given an opportunity to solve the problem and the government should step in only if necessary. Mr. Thompson reviewed challenges he had given to industry at the FTC's spyware

Industry Positions

At a hearing before the Senate Commerce, Science, and Transportation Committee's Communications Subcommittee on March 23, 2004, witnesses discussed the difficulties in legislating in an area where definitions are unclear, and that the pace of technology might quickly render any such definitions obsolete. Robert Holleyman, representing the Business Software Alliance, testified that the focus of legislation should be regulating bad behavior, not technology. He expressed reservations about legislation which then was pending in the Senate, and called on Congress not to preclude the evolution of tools and marketplace solutions to the problem.

While there is concern generally about any software product installed without the user's knowledge or consent, adware is a particular area of controversy. Many users object to pop-up ads as vigorously as they do to spam. The extent to which pop-up ads are, or should be, included in a definition of spyware was discussed at the 2004 Senate Commerce subcommittee hearing. Avi Naider, President and CEO of WhenU.com, argued that although his company's WhenU software does create popup ads, it is not spyware because users are notified that the program is about to be installed, must affirmatively consent to a license agreement, and may decline it. Mr. Naider explained that his program often is "bundled" with software that users obtain for free (called "free-ware"), or a software developer may offer users a choice between paying for the software or obtaining it for free if they agree to receive ads from WhenU. While agreeing that spyware is a serious concern, and that Congress and the FTC should regulate in this area, Mr. Naider urged that legislation be written carefully to exclude products like his that offer notice and choice and therefore should not be considered spyware. As noted above, WhenU has filed suit against a Utah law regulating spyware.

At the 2004 House Energy and Commerce subcommittee hearing, David Baker, representing Earthlink, described his company's efforts to combat spyware, and supported legislation to protect consumers. Jeffrey Friedberg, from Microsoft, said that his company supports a "holistic" solution, and that if existing law is inadequate, then additional legislation would be appropriate.

The House Energy and Commerce Committee held another hearing on January 26, 2005. At the hearing, representatives of Microsoft and Earthlink generally supported H.R. 29, with some minor alterations. Modifications were made to that bill during subcommittee and full committee markup, reportedly in response to industry and Senate concerns. [30] Not all industry representatives support the bill, however. The Information Technology Association of America (ITAA), for example, reportedly is backing H.R. 744 instead [31] (that bill is summarized below).

Consumer Groups and Others

At the 2004 Senate Commerce subcommittee hearing, John L. Levine, author of *The Internet for Dummies* and similar books, concluded that legislation should ban spyware entirely, or consumers should be able to give a one-time permanent notice (akin to the telemarketing Do Not Call list) that they do not want spyware on their computers. He also said that the legislation should allow consumers to sue violators, rather than relying only on the FTC and state Attorneys General to enforce the law.

At the same 2004 hearing, CDT's Jerry Berman noted that three existing laws can be used to address spyware concerns: the Federal Trade Commission Act (the FTC Act), the Electronic Communications Privacy Act (ECPA), and the Computer Fraud and Abuse Act (CFAA). He added that technology measures, self-regulation and user education also are important to dealing with spyware. He concluded that CDT believes that new legislation specifically targeted at spyware would be useful, but that Congress also should pass broad Internet privacy legislation that could address the privacy aspects of the spyware debate. Another CDT representative, Ari Schwartz, made similar arguments at the April 2004 and January 2005 House Energy and Commerce hearings.

109th Congress Legislation

Two bills are pending in the House — H.R. 29 (Bono) and H.R. 744 (Goodlatte) — both of which are very similar to legislation that passed the House in 2004 (H.R. 2929 and H.R. 4661, respectively). One bill is pending in the Senate — S. 687 (Burns), which is similar to legislation that was considered in 2004, but did not reach the floor (S. 2145). Action in the 108th Congress is summarized in the Appendix.

The House Energy and Commerce Committee held a hearing on H.R. 29 on January 26, 2005. H.R. 774 was referred to the House Judiciary Committee; no hearing has been held on that bill. S. 687 was referred to the Senate Commerce, Science, and Transportation Committee; no hearing has been held.

H.R. 29 (Bono), Spy Act

H.R. 29, the Securely Protect Yourself Against Cyber Trespass Act (Spy Act), is a revised version of H.R. 2929, which passed the House in 2004 (see Appendix). The only change made to the bill's language when it was reintroduced was changing the date when the act would sunset to 2010 (instead of 2009) so that it still would have a five-year lifetime. Other modifications (including changing SPY ACT to Spy Act) were made during subcommittee markup CRS-11 on February 4, 2005, and full committee markup on March 9, 2005, when the bill was ordered reported.

The provisions of H.R. 29 as ordered reported are summarized in general below. *Significant additions or deletions that occurred during the two markups are shown in italics.* Different sections have various effective dates, but the legislation overall would expire on December 31, 2010.

- Section 2 prohibits deceptive acts or practices relating to spyware. It would be unlawful for anyone who is not the owner or authorized user (hereafter, the user) of a protected computer to —
  - take control of the computer by: utilizing the computer to send unsolicited information or material from the computer to others; diverting the computer's browser away from the site the user intended to view without authorization of the owner or authorized user of the computer, or otherwise authorized; accessing, *hijacking,* or using the computer's Internet connection and thereby damaging the computer or causing the owner, user, *or third party defrauded by such conduct,* to incur unauthorized financial charges *or other costs*; using the

computer as part of an activity performed by a group of computers that causes damage to another computer; or delivering advertisements that a user cannot close without turning off the computer or closing all sessions of the Internet browser;
- modify settings related to use of the computer or the computer's access to the Internet by altering the Web page that appears when the browser is launched; the default provider used to access or search the Internet; the list of bookmarks; or security or other settings that protect information about the user for the purposes of causing damage or harm to the computer or its owner or user;
- collect personally identifiable information through keylogging;
- *induce the owner or user of a computer to disclose PII by means of a Web page that is substantially similar to a Web page established or provided by another person, or mislead the owner or user that such Web page is provided by such other person;*
- induce the user to install software, or prevent reasonable efforts to block the installation or execution of, or to disable, software, by presenting the user with an option to decline installation but the installation nevertheless proceeds, or causing software that has been properly removed or disabled to automatically reinstall or reactivate;
- misrepresent that certain actions or information is needed to open, view, or play a particular type of content;
- misrepresent the identity or authority of a person or entity providing software in order to induce the user to install or execute the software;
- misrepresent the identity of a person seeking information in order to induce the user to provide personally identifiable password or account information, or without the authority of the intended recipient of the information;
- remove, disable, or render inoperative security, anti-spyware, or anti-virus technology installed on the computer;
- install or execute on the computer one or more additional software components with the intent of causing a person to use such component in a way that violates any other provision of this section.

- Section 3 prohibits the collection of certain information without notice and consent. It contains an opt-in requirement, whereby it would be unlawful —
  - to transmit any information collection program without obtaining consent from the user unless notice was provided as required in this bill, and the program included certain functions required in the bill; or
  - to execute any information collection functions installed on a computer, without obtaining consent from the user before the information collection program was executed.

"Information collection program" is defined as software that collects personally identifiable information and sends it to a person other than the user, or uses such information to deliver or display advertising; or collects information regarding Web pages accessed using the computer and uses such information to deliver or display advertising, *except if the only information collected regarding Web pages is information regarding Web pages within a particular Web site and such information is not sent to anyone other than the provider of that Web site or a party authorized to facilitate the display or functionality of Web pages within that Web site, and the only advertising delivered to or displayed using such information is advertising on Web pages within that particular Web site.* The bill specifies certain requirements for notice (differentiating among various types of software at issue) and consent.

Only one clear and conspicuous notice, in plain language, is required if multiple collection programs, provided together or as a suite of functionally-related software, executed any of the information collection functions. The user must be notified, and consent obtained, before the program is used to collect or send information of a type, or for a purpose, materially different from and outside the scope of what was stated in an initial or previous notice. No subsequent notification is otherwise required. Users must be able to disable or remove the information collection program without undue effort or knowledge. If an information collection program uses the collected information to display advertisements when the owner or user accesses a Web page or online location other than that of the program's provider, the program must include a function that identifies itself, *except for the embedded display of advertising on a Web page that contemporaneously displays other information.* Telecommunications carriers, information service or interactive computer service providers, cable operators, or providers of transmission capability are not liable under the act.

- Section 4 directs the FTC to enforce the act, and the FTC is either directed or permitted to promulgate rules for various sections.

  Violations are to be treated as an unfair or deceptive act or practice under the section 18 of the FTC Act. The FTC may seek a civil penalty (maximum of $3 million per violation) if a person engages in a pattern or practice of violations. Any single action, or conduct that affects multiple computers, is to be treated as a single violation. But a single action or conduct that violates multiple sections of the act is CRS-13 to be treated as multiple violations. *Civil penalties may not be granted by the FTC or a court, however, unless it is established that the action was committed with actual knowledge, or knowledge fairly implied on the basis of objective circumstances, that such act is unfair or deceptive, or violates this act.* [The bill as introduced said that violations that were committed with actual knowledge, or knowledge fairly implied on the basis of objective circumstances, would be treated as unfair or deceptive acts or practices violating a rule promulgated under section 18 of the FTC Act, rather than saying that penalties may only be granted if those conditions are met]. *In determining the amount of any penalty, the court shall take into account the degree of culpability, any history of prior such conduct, ability to pay, affect on ability to continue to do business, and such other matters as justice may require.*

- Other sections include —
  - Exceptions for a variety of law enforcement/national security-related activities, and for network providers that use monitoring software to protect network security and prevent fraud.
  - Liability protection for manufacturers or retailers of computer equipment if they are providing third party-branded software that is installed on the equipment being manufactured or sold.
  - Provisions under which the act supersedes state laws that expressly regulate deceptive conduct similar to that described in the act, or the transmission or execution of a computer program similar to that described in the act, or computer software that displays advertising content based on Web pages accessed using a computer. No person other than a state Attorney General is allowed to bring a civil action under any state law if that action is premised, in whole or in part, on violations of this bill, except that this bill does not limit the enforcement of any state consumer protection law. The bill

does not preempt other state trespass, contract, or tort laws, or other state laws to the extent they relate to fraud. And,

- Requirements for the FTC to submit an annual report about its actions based on the bill, and a second report. The second report is to be on the use of "cookies, including tracking cookies" to deliver or display advertisements, the methods by which cookies and the websites that place them on websites function separately and together, and comparing the use of cookies with the use of information collection programs to determine the extent to which such uses are similar or different. The report may include recommendations including treatment of cookies under this act or other laws. [*Regarding the second report, the original bill said the report was to be on "tracking cookies," not on cookies generically, and on the extent to which tracking cookies were covered by this act, without a comparison of cookies and information collection programs.*]

In general, the FTC is required to issue regulations required by the act no later than six months after enactment, *and shall determine that the regulations are consistent with the public interest and the purposes of the act*

H.R. 774 (Goodlatte), I-SPY Act

The Internet Spyware Prevention (I-SPY Act) was introduced on February 10, 2005, and referred to the House Judiciary Committee. The bill is identical to H.R. 4661 as it passed the House in 2004, except that the four years for which funding is authorized is shifted from FY2005-2008, to FY2006-2009. H.R. 774 would make it illegal to access a computer without authorization to obtain sensitive personal information or cause damage to the computer, and imposes fines and sentences up to two years in prison. If the unauthorized access is to further another federal crime, a sentence of up to five years is allowed. No person may bring a civil action under state law if the action is premised in whole or in part upon a violation of this bill. The bill authorizes $10 million for each of four fiscal years (FY2006-FY2009) to the Department of Justice for prosecutions needed to discourage spyware and "phishing." [32] Language is included clarifying that the bill does not prohibit any lawfully authorized investigative, protective, or intelligence activities.

S. 687 (Burns), SPY BLOCK Act

The Software Principles Yielding Better Levels of Consumer Knowledge Act, was introduced by Senator Burns on March 20, 2005. It is similar, but not identical, to S. 2145 from the 108th Congress (see Appendix). The bill would make it unlawful for a person who is not an authorized user of a computer —

- to cause the installation of software on that computer in a manner that conceals from the user the fact that the software was being installed, or prevents the user from having an opportunity to knowingly grant or withhold consent to the installation. This does not apply to (1) the installation of software falling within the scope of a previous grant of authorization, (2) installation of an upgrade to software already installed with the user's authorization, (3) software installed before the first retail sale and delivery of the computer, or (4) installation of software that ceases to operate when the user of the computer exits the software or service through which the user accesses the Internet, if the software so installed does not begin to operate again when the user accesses the Internet in the future.
- to induce a person to consent to the installation of software by means of a materially false or misleading representation concerning — the identity of the operator of an Internet website or online service where the software is made available for download from the Internet; the identity of the author, publisher, or authorized distributor of the software, the nature or function of the software; or the consequences of not installing the software. The software must be able to be easily uninstalled or disabled, with exceptions (for example, a parent, employee, or system administrator may install software that another user would find difficult to uninstall or disable)to
- to cause the installation of software that includes a surreptitious information collection feature (as defined in the legislation), or to use such software to collect information about a user of the computer or how the computer is used. This does not, however, prohibit a person from causing the installation of software that collects and transmits only information that is reasonably needed to determine whether or not the user of a computer is licensed or authorized to use the software.
- to cause the installation of "adware" that does not have a label or other reasonable means of identifying which software caused the advertisement to be displayed. This would not apply if the advertisement is displayed only when a user is accessing an Internet website or online

service operated by the publisher of the software, or that operator has provided express consent to the display of such advertisements to users of the website or service. It also would not apply if the advertisement is displayed only in a manner, or at a time, such that a reasonable user would understand which software caused the delivery of the advertisement.

- to engage in an unfair and deceptive act or practice that involves utilizing the computer to send unsolicited information or material to other computers; to divert an authorized user's Internet browser away from the site the user intended to view; to display an advertisement or other content through windows in an Internet browser in such a manner that the computer's user cannot end the display without turning off the computer or terminating the browser; modify computer settings related to use of the computer or Internet access, such as altering the default website that initially appears when a user opens an Internet browser; or remove, disable, or render inoperative a security or privacy protection technology installed on the computer.

The bill also provides liability limitations. For example, a person would not violate the law solely by providing an Internet connection through which spyware was installed. Network or online service providers to which an authorized user subscribes would not violate the section on collection of information, for example, if they do so to protect the security of the network, service or computer. Computer manufacturers and retailers would not be liable for third-party branded software unless they use a surreptitious information collection feature included in the software to collect information about a user of the computer or the use of the computer or knows that the software will cause advertisements for the manufacturer or retailer to be displayed. Furthermore, nothing in the Act prohibits any lawfully authorized investigative, protective, or intelligence activity of a law enforcement agency.

The FTC is allowed to issue rules that are necessary to implement or clarify the provisions of the Act, including regulations establishing safe harbors, such as notifications or labels that are sufficient to avoid violations. The FTC may establish additional liability limitations beyond those provided in the Act.

Generally, the FTC is to enforce the law as if a violation was an unfair or deceptive practice. However, other agencies were identified for enforcing the law for certain businesses (e.g., the Comptroller of the Currency would enforce it for national banks and federal branches and federal agencies of foreign banks). State Attorneys General may bring actions on behalf of residents of that state, but must notify the FTC, and the FTC may intervene. The Act supersedes state laws or laws of political subdivisions of that state if the law expressly limits or restricts the installation or use of software to collect information about the user or the user's activities, or causes advertisements to be delivered to the user, except to the extent that any such statute, regulation, or rule prohibits deception in connection with the installation or use of such software. It supersedes any statute, regulation, or rule of a state or political subdivision thereof that prescribes specific methods for providing notification before the installation of software on a computer. It does not preempt the applicability of state criminal, trespass, contract, tort, or anti-fraud law. Criminal penalties (fines and/or imprisonment of up to five years) are set for violation of the law. The law would become effective 180 days after enactment.

APPENDIX: SUMMARY OF LEGISLATIVE ACTION IN THE 108TH CONGRESS

The House passed two spyware bills in the 108th Congress — H.R. 2929 and H.R. 4661. The Senate Commerce Committee reported S. 2145 (Burns), amended, December 9, 2004 (S.Rept. 108-424). None of these bills cleared that Congress.

The Senate Commerce, Science, and Transportation Committee's Subcommittee on Communications held a hearing on spyware on March 23, 2004. The House Energy and Commerce's Subcommittee on Telecommunications and the Internet held a hearing on April 29, 2004. The House passed two spyware bills (H.R. 2929 and H.R. 4661) and the Senate Commerce Committee reported S. 2145, but there was no further action.

Media sources reported prior to the House votes that the two House bills would be combined into a single package, but they were not. *Congressional Quarterly* explained that the two bills represent different philosophies about how to deal with the spyware issue: "Some want to crack down on the so-called bad actors who use spyware for nefarious purposes. Others propose requiring anybody installing the software to get a computer user's advance permission." [33] The first approach is that taken in H.R. 4661; the second is in H.R. 2929.

H.R. 2929 (Bono), SPY ACT

H.R. 2929 has been reintroduced in the 109th Congress as H.R. 29, which is discussed above.

In the 108th Congress, the Securely Protect Yourself Against Cyber Trespass Act (SPY ACT) passed the House (399-1) on October 5, 2004. As passed, H.R. 2929 included the following provisions. Different sections had various effective dates, but the legislation overall would have expired on December 31, 2009. The version passed by the House reflected changes to the committee-reported version made by a manager's amendment.

- Section 2 would have prohibited deceptive acts or practices relating to spyware. It would have been unlawful for anyone who was not the owner or authorized user (hereafter, the user) of a protected computer to —
  - take control of the computer by: utilizing the computer to send unsolicited information or material from the computer to others; diverting the computer's browser away from the site the user intended to view without authorization of the owner or authorized user of the computer, or otherwise authorized; accessing or using the computer's Internet connection and thereby damaging the computer or causing the user to incur unauthorized financial charges; using the computer as part of an activity performed by a group of computers that causes damage to another computer; or CRS-18 delivering advertisements that a user cannot close without turning off the computer or closing all sessions of the Internet browser;
  - modify settings related to use of the computer or the computer's access to the Internet by altering the Web page that appears when the browser is launched; the default provider used to access or search the Internet; the list of bookmarks; or security or other settings that protect information about the user for the purposes of causing damage or harm to the computer or its owner or user;
  - collect personally identifiable information through keylogging;
  - induce the user to install software, or prevent reasonable efforts to block the installation or execution of, or to disable, software, by presenting the user with an option to decline installation but the installation nevertheless proceeds, or causing software that has been properly removed or disabled to automatically reinstall or reactivate;

- misrepresent that certain actions or information is needed to open, view, or play a particular type of content;
- misrepresent the identity or authority of a person or entity providing software in order to induce the user to install or execute the software;
- misrepresent the identity of a person seeking information in order to induce the user to provide personally identifiable password or account information, or without the authority of the intended recipient of the information;
- remove, disable, or render inoperative security, anti-spyware, or anti-virus technology installed on the computer;
- install or execute on the computer one or more additional software components with the intent of causing a person to use such component in a way that violates any other provision of this section.

- Section 3 would have prohibited the collection of certain information without notice and consent. It contained an opt-in requirement, whereby it would have been unlawful —
  - to transmit any information collection program without obtaining consent from the user unless notice was provided as required in this bill, and the program included certain functions required in the bill;
  - or to execute any information collection functions installed on a computer, without obtaining consent from the user before the information collection program was executed.

"Information collection program" was defined as software that collects personally identifiable information and sends it to a person other than the user, or uses such information to deliver or display advertising; or collects information regarding Web pages accessed using the computer and uses such information to deliver or display advertising. The bill specified certain requirements for notice (differentiating among various types of software at issue) and consent.

Only one clear and conspicuous notice, in plain language, was required if multiple collection programs, provided together or as a suite of functionally-related software, executed any of the information collection functions. The user had to be notified, and consent obtained, before the program was used to collect or send information of a type, or for a purpose, materially different from and outside the scope of what was stated in an initial or previous notice. No subsequent notification was otherwise required.

Users had to be able to disable or remove the information collection program without undue effort or knowledge. If an information collection program used the collected information to display advertisements when the owner or user accessed a Web page or online location other than that of the program's provider, the program had to include a function that identified itself. Telecommunications carriers, information service or interactive computer service providers, cable operators, or providers of transmission capability were not liable under the act.

- Section 4 directed the FTC to enforce the act, and the FTC was either directed or permitted to promulgate rules for various sections.

Civil penalties were set for various violations of the law or related regulations. Violations committed with actual knowledge, or knowledge fairly implied on the basis of objective circumstances, that such act was unfair or deceptive, or violated this act, were to be treated as an unfair or deceptive act or practice under the FTC Act. The FTC could have sought a civil penalty (maximum of $3 million per violation) if a person engaged in a pattern or practice of violations. Any single action, or conduct that affected multiple computers, was to be treated as a single violation. But a single action or conduct that violated multiple sections of the act was to be treated as multiple violations.

- Other sections included —
  - Exceptions for a variety of law enforcement/national security-related activities, and for network providers that use monitoring software to protect network security and prevent fraud.
  - Liability protection for manufacturers or retailers of computer equipment if they are providing third party-branded software that is installed on the equipment being manufactured or sold.
  - Provisions under which the act supersedes state laws that expressly regulate deceptive conduct similar to that described in the act, or the transmission or execution of a computer program similar to that described in the act, or computer software that displays advertising content based on Web pages accessed using a computer. No person other than a state Attorney General would have been allowed to bring a civil action under any state law if that action was premised, in whole or in part, on violations of this bill, except that this bill did not limit the enforcement of any state consumer protection law.

The bill would not have preempted other state trespass, contract, or tort laws, or other state laws to the extent they relate to fraud. And,

- Requirements for the FTC to submit an annual report about its actions based on the bill, and, separately, a report on the use of "tracking cookies" to display advertisements and the extent to which they are covered by this bill.

H.R. 4661 (Goodlatte), I-SPY Act

The Internet Spyware Prevention Act passed the House on October 7, 2004 (415-0). The bill would have made it illegal to access a computer without authorization to obtain sensitive personal information or cause damage to the computer, and imposed fines and sentences up to two years in prison. If the unauthorized access was to further another federal crime, a sentence of up to five years was allowed. No person could have brought a civil action under state law if the action was premised in whole or in part upon a violation of this bill. The bill authorized $10 million for each of four fiscal years (FY2005-FY2008) to the Department of Justice for prosecutions needed to discourage spyware and "phishing." [34] Language was included clarifying that the bill did not prohibit any lawfully authorized investigative, protective, or intelligence activities.

S. 2145 (Burns), SPY BLOCK Act

The Software Principles Yielding Better Levels of Consumer Knowledge Act, was ordered reported from the Senate Commerce Committee on September 22, 2004, after adopting a Burns substitute amendment that "steered clear of setting technical requirements for software companies." [35] Another amendment, offered by Senator Allen, was adopted that sets criminal penalties for spyware providers. The bill was reported, without a written report, on November 19, 2004, and with a written report (S.Rept. 108-424) on December 7. There was no floor action. The bill, as reported, would have made it unlawful for a person who is not an authorized user of a computer —

- to cause the installation of software on a computer in a manner designed to conceal from the user the fact that the software was being installed, or prevent the user from having an opportunity to knowingly grant or withhold consent to the installation. This would not have applied to software falling within the scope of a previous grant of authorization, installation of an upgrade to software already

installed with the user's authorization, or software installed before the first retail sale of the computer.
- to induce a person to consent to the installation of software by means of a materially false or misleading representation concerning — the identity of the operator of an Internet Website or online service where the software is made available for download from the Internet; the identity of the author or publisher of the software, the nature or function of the software; or the consequences of not installing the software. The software had to be able to be easily uninstalled or disabled, with exceptions (for example, a parent or system administrator may install software that another user would find difficult to uninstall or disable).
- to authorize or cause the installation of software that collects information about the user of the computer or the user's activities and transmits that information to any other person on an automatic basis or at the direction of someone other than the authorized user, with exceptions.
- to authorize or cause the installation of "adware."
- to knowingly and without authorization use the computer to send unsolicited information or material to other computers; to divert an authorized user's Internet browser away from the site the user intended to view; to display an advertisement or other content through windows in an Internet browser in such a manner that the computer's user cannot end the display without turning off the computer or terminating the browser; covertly modify computer settings related to use of the computer or Internet access, such as altering the default website that initially appears when a user opens an Internet browser; use software installed in violation of an earlier section of the bill regarding collection of information; or remove, disable, or render inoperative a security or privacy protection technology installed on the computer.

The bill also would have provided liability limitations for certain persons. For example, a person would not have violated the law solely by providing an Internet connection through which spyware was installed. Network or online service providers to which an authorized user subscribes would not have been deemed to have violated the section on collection of information, for example, if they did so to protect the security of the network, service or computer.

Generally, the FTC would have enforced the law as an unfair or deceptive practice. However, other agencies were identified for enforcing the law for certain businesses (e.g., the Comptroller of the Currency would enforce it for national banks and federal branches and federal agencies of foreign banks).

State Attorneys General could have brought actions on behalf of residents of that state, but would have been required to notify the FTC, and the FTC could intervene. The law would have superseded state laws or laws of political subdivisions of that state if the law expressly limited or restricted the installation or use of software to collect information about the user or the user's activities, or cause advertisements to be delivered to the user, except to the extent that any such statute, regulation, or rule prohibited deception in connection with the installation or use of such software. It would not have preempted the applicability of state trespass, contract, tort, or anti-fraud law. Criminal penalties (fines and/or imprisonment of up to five years) were set for violations of the law

REFERENCES

[1] Testimony to the Senate Committee on Commerce, Science, and Transportation, Subcommittee on Communications, March 23, 2004. Available on CDT's spyware site [http://www.cdt.org/privacy/spyware/] along with a November 2003 CDT report entitled Ghosts in Our Machines: Background and Policy Proposals on the "Spyware" Problem.

[2] The existence of keylogging software was publicly highlighted in 2001 when the FBI, with a search warrant, installed such software on a suspect's computer, allowing them to obtain his password for an encryption program he used, and thereby evidence. Some privacy advocates argued that wiretapping authority should have been obtained, but the judge, after reviewing classified information about how the software works, ruled in favor of the FBI. Press reports also indicate that the FBI is developing a "Magic Lantern" program that performs a similar task, but can be installed on a subject's computer remotely by surreptitiously including it in an e-mail message, for example.

[3] For more on identity theft, see CRS Report RS22082, Identity Theft: The Internet Connection, by Marcia S. Smith; and CRS Report RL31919, Remedies Available to Victims of Identity Theft, by Angie A. Welborn.

[4] According to its website [http://www.staysafeonline.info], NCSA is a public-private partnership, with government sponsors including the Department of Homeland Security and the FTC. Its Board of Officers includes representatives from Cisco Systems, Symantec, RSA Security, AOL, McAfee, Microsoft, and BellSouth.

[5] Largest In-Home Study of Home Computer Users Shows Major Online Threats, Perception Gap. Business Wire, October 25, 2004, 08:02 (via Factiva). The study is available on NCSA's website at [http://www.staysafeonline.info/news/safety_study_v04.pdf].

[6] Spyware Infiltration Rises in Corporate Networks, but Webroot Survey Finds Companies Still Neglect Threat. PR Newswire, October 27, 2004, 06:00 (via Factiva).

[7] Cha, Ariana Eunjung. Computer Users Face New Scourge; Hidden Adware Programs Hijack Hard Drives. Washington Post, October 10, 2004, p. A1 (via Factiva).

[8] Available at [http://www.ftc.gov/bcp/conline/pubs/alerts/spywarealrt.htm].

[9] For example, see Bass, Steve. Spyware Wrap-Up. PC World, November 3, 2004. Available at [http://www.pcworld.com/howto/article/0,aid,118215,00.asp]. The September 2004 issue of Consumer Reports rates anti-spyware products

[10] The transcript of the workshop is available at [http://www.ftc.gov/bcp/workshops/spyware/transcript.pdf].

[11] House Energy and Commerce Committee. Hearing, April 29, 2004. Hearing transcript provided by Federal Document Clearing House (via Factiva)

[12] An FTC press release, and a link to the report, are at [http://www.ftc.gov/opa/2005/03/spywarerpt.htm].

[13] FTC Cracks Down on Spyware Operation. FTC press release, October 12, 2004. [http://www.ftc.gov/opa/2004/10/spyware.htm].

[14] FTC press release, Ibid.

[15] Wang, Beverly. New Hampshire Man Denies Wrongdoing in Federal Anti-Spam Case. Associated Press, October 8, 2004, 20:52 (via Factiva).

[16] Federal Judge Orders Immediate Halt to Spyware. Associated Press, October 23, 2004, 14:40 (via Factiva).

[17] House Committee on Energy and Commerce. Hearing, April 29, 2004. Hearing transcript provided by the Federal Document Clearing House (via Factiva).

[18] See [http://www.le.state.ut.us/~2004/bills/hbillenr/hb0323.pdf] for the enrolled text of the law.
[19] Tech Companies Lobby Utah Governor Against Broad Anti-Spyware Bill. Warren's Washington Internet Daily, March 22, 2004 (via Factiva).
[20] Utah Anti-Spyware Bill Opposed by High-Tech Becomes Law. Warren's Washington Internet Daily, March 25, 2004 (via Factiva).
[21] Wallace, Brice. Deseret Morning News, April 22, 2004, E01 (via Factiva).
[22] Judge Grants NY Pop-Up Company Preliminary Injunction Against Spyware Law. Associated Press, June 23, 2004, 06:06 (via Factiva).
[23] California Business and Professions Code. Section 22947-22947.6. Available at: [http://www.leginfo.ca.gov/cgi-bin/waisgate?WAISdocID=6431619090+0+0+0&WAISaction=retrieve]
[24] California Goes After Spyware. Reuters, October 2, 2004., 07:17 am, available at : [http://www.wired.com/news/politics/0,1283,65203,00.html]
[25] See CRS Report RL31953, "Spam": An Overview of Issues Concerning Commercial Electronic Mail, by Marcia S. Smith.
[26] MX Logic Reports Compliance with Anti-Spam Law Increased 6 Percent in November; Highest Monthly Compliance to Date. Press release, December 13, 2004. [http://www.mxlogic.com/news_events/12_13_04.html]
[27] As reported in: "Walk Slowly" on Privacy Legislation, FTC Comr. Says. Warren's Washington Internet Daily, March 7, 2005 (via Factiva).
[28] A video of the presentation is available at [http://www.cato.org/event.php?eventid=1725]. See also: FTC's Swindle: Leave Spyware Solution to Industry. Warren's Washington Internet Daily, November 8, 2004 (via Factiva).
[29] House Energy and Commerce Committee. Hearing, April 29, 2004. Hearing transcript provided by Federal Document Clearing House (via Factiva). workshop: to develop a set of "best practices ... including meaningful notice and choice so that consumers can make informed decisions about whether or not they wish to deal with an online business that uses monitoring software or partners with companies that do"; to develop a campaign to educate consumers and businesses about spyware and how to cope with it; and to establish a mechanism to allow businesses and consumers to have a dialog "on how government

can take action against those who do wrong and undermine consumer confidence through the misuse of spyware."

[30] Juliana Gruenwald. House Panel Backs Bill to Crack Down on Spyware. Technology Daily, available at [http://nationaljournal.com/members/markups/2005/02/200504702.htm].

[31] Amol Sharma. House Committee Approves Bono's Anti-Spyware Bill. CQ Today, March 9, 2005, 12:19 pm.

[32] "Phishing" refers to an Internet-based practice in which someone misrepresents their identity or authority in order to induce another person to provide personally identifiable information (PII).

[33] Sharma, Amol. Congressional "Spyware" Fix Likely to Prove Elusive. CQ Weekly, October 9, 2004, p. 2377.

[34] "Phishing" refers to an Internet-based practice in which someone misrepresents their identity or authority in order to induce another person to provide personally identifiable information (PII).

[35] Senate Panel Approves 'Spyware' Bill. CQ Weekly, September 25, 2004, p. 2273.

Chapter 2

MONITORING SOFTWARE ON YOUR PC: SPYWARE, ADWARE, AND OTHER SOFTWARE[*]

Staff Report

INTRODUCTION

On April 19, 2004, the Federal Trade Commission (FTC) [1] sponsored *Monitoring Software on Your PC: Spyware, Adware, and Other Software*, a one-day public workshop to explore the issues associated with computer software known as "spyware." [2] The workshop featured six panels made up of 34 representatives from the computer industry, the electronic advertising industry, anti-spyware product industry, trade associations, government agencies, consumer and privacy advocacy groups, and other interested parties. Panel topics included:

- Defining, Understanding, and Disseminating Spyware;
- Security Risks and PC Functionality;
- Privacy Risks;
- Industry Responses to Spyware – Industry Best Practices and Working with the Government;
- Technological Responses to Spyware; and

---

[*] Excerpted from Spyware Workshop dated March 2005.

- Government Responses to Spyware – Law Enforcement, Consumer Education, and Coordinating with Industry.

One purpose of the workshop was to broaden the FTC's understanding of the information practices of the online marketplace and their impact on consumers, and to continue the FTC's longstanding tradition of facilitating initiatives that foster privacy protection and security. The workshop also was intended to provide information that would inform the public debate over spyware and assist government, businesses, and consumers in developing effective responses to spyware.[3]

FTC staff has prepared this report to present information concerning the issues discussed at the workshop. Part I of the report provides an overview of the issues the report covers and a summary of FTC staff's conclusions. Part II discusses defining spyware, how it is distributed, and the challenge of uninstalling spyware from computers. Part III describes the effects of spyware, including its impact on computer performance and its creation of privacy and security risks. Part IV discusses industry efforts to address spyware through technological innovation, self-regulation, and consumer education. Part V describes government efforts to address spyware through law enforcement, legislation, and consumer education measures. Part VI provides a brief conclusion.

As explained in detail below, based on the information received in connection with the workshop[4] and other available information, FTC staff concludes:

- It is difficult to define spyware with precision. The working definition proposed for purposes of the workshop was software that aids in gathering information about a person or organization without their knowledge and which may send such information to another entity without the consumer's consent, or asserts control over a computer without the consumer's knowledge. Panelists and commenters agreed that this was a useful starting point for defining spyware.
- However, the workshop discussions also highlighted additional challenges in defining spyware relating to what constitutes adequate consent, and what constitutes sufficient harm to merit software being labeled spyware. In FTC staff's view, a consensus definition of spyware cannot be developed until fundamental issues concerning consent and harm are resolved.

- Spyware is distributed in the same ways as other software; it can be downloaded from the Internet, bundled with other software, transferred via peer-to-peer ("P2P") filesharing networks, installed from CDs, or pre-installed on new computers. In addition, spyware may be distributed by instant messaging, emails, or web pages.
- Spyware is a serious and growing problem.
- Spyware can impair the operation of computers, causing them to crash and interfering with the ability of consumers to use them.
- Spyware, especially keystroke loggers, can create substantial privacy risks.
- Spyware can assert control over computers, and use that control to create security risks and cause other harms.
- Spyware often is more difficult to uninstall than other types of software.
- The incidence of spyware can be decreased if the private sector and the government act, separately and in concert.
- Technological solutions – firewalls, anti-spyware software, and improved browsers and operating systems – can provide significant protection to consumers from the risks related to spyware.
- Industry should: (1) develop standards for defining spyware and disclosing information about it to consumers; (2) expand efforts to educate consumers about spyware risks; and (3) assist law enforcement efforts.
- Government should: (1) increase criminal and civil prosecution under existing laws of those who distribute spyware; (2) increase efforts to educate consumers about the risks of spyware; and (3) encourage technological solutions.

DEFINING AND UNDERSTANDING SPYWARE AND ITS DISTRIBUTION

Defining Spyware

The first issue discussed at the workshop was the definition of "spyware." Despite its recent vintage, the etymology of "spyware" is unclear. Until 1999, it appears that the term was used to refer to monitoring equipment such as small cameras.[5] "Spyware" first began to be used in the computer software context in 1999 when Zone Labs used it in a press release for its Zone Alarm firewall product.[6]

In 2000, Gibson Research launched the first anti-spyware product, OptOut. Steve Gibson, the developer of OptOut, described spyware as "any software that employs a user's Internet connection in the background (the so-called 'backchannel') without their knowledge or explicit permission."[7] The term "spyware" thus apparently was used at the outset to refer to software that was installed without the knowledge and consent of users and that operated surreptitiously.

Spyware has evolved to have a variety of meanings.[8] Panelists generally agreed that reaching an industry consensus on one definition has been elusive because of the technical complexity and dynamic nature of software.[9] Several panelists observed that it is also difficult to define spyware because consumers and the business community may differ on what they believe is appropriate behavior in distributing software and because harmful software may cause a wide variety of problems.[10]

Challenges in Defining Spyware

Panelists identified three main conceptual challenges in reaching a consensus definition of spyware. The first challenge concerns knowledge and consent. There appears to be general agreement that software should be considered "spyware" only if it is downloaded or installed on a computer without the user's knowledge and consent.[11] However, unresolved issues remain concerning how, what, and when consumers need to be told about software installed on their computers for consent to be adequate.[12] For instance, distributors often disclose in an End User Licensing Agreement (EULA) that there is additional software bundled with primary software, but some panelists and commenters did not view such disclosure as sufficient to infer consent to the installation of the bundled software.[13]

Second, another question is whether the definition should limit "spyware" to software that monitors and collects data relating to computer use. Such a definition would be consistent with the fundamental concept that the software must "spy" on computer users.[14] However, it presumably would not include software that does not collect data but adversely affects computer performance or otherwise interferes with the use of computers.[15]

A final challenge in reaching consensus on the definition of spyware is determining the nature and extent of harm that the software must cause. For instance, some would treat software that "trespasses" on a computer as spyware because they consider trespass to be *per se* harmful,[16] even if the software is otherwise benign or beneficial. In contrast, there was general consensus throughout the workshop that software should cause some harm to users before being labeled spyware. There was disagreement, however, as to the type and magnitude of injury needed to meet this definition.[17]

Classifying Adware as Spyware[18]

In FTC staff's view, adware aptly illustrates the challenges associated with developing a workable definition of spyware. Adware is often bundled with other software programs, which are frequently provided to consumers for free. Some types of adware monitor computer use (including websites visited), analyze that information to determine ads in which the users might be interested, and then display targeted ads to users based on this analysis.[19] On the other hand, other types of adware do not monitor computer use and instead just serve advertising messages to users.[20]

Workshop panelists and commenters stated a range of views as to whether and when adware should be classified as spyware. Some panelists argued that adware is spyware if users have not received clear notice about what the software will do or have not provided adequate consent to its installation or operation.[21] In turn, some types of adware would not meet some definitions of spyware because they do not monitor computer use.[22] Other workshop participants apparently would view adware as spyware if it causes consumers to receive pop-up ads,[23] regardless of whether consumers are bombarded with such ads or just occasionally receive such ads.

Legislative and Regulatory Definitions of Spyware

Because of the challenges of developing a workable definition of spyware, nearly all panelists expressed the concern that legislation or regulations tied to a definition of the term "spyware" might define the term so broadly that it would inadvertently cover some types of beneficial or benign software.[24] One panelist stated that overly broad legislative definitions might inadvertently regulate software that many users depend upon for a safe Internet experience.[25] In his view, for example, parental control software might be considered spyware under a recently enacted Utah statute.[26] This statute might also treat security programs that banks and financial institutions use to monitor and protect access to their online services as spyware.[27]

Because of the concern that a legislative or regulatory definition of spyware might be too broad, a number of panelists and commenters observed that it would be more productive to identify and prohibit unfair or deceptive practices associated with software.[28] Panelists expressed broad support for the Consumer Software Working Group's effort to identify and prevent specific activities related to software that are unfair, deceptive, or devious.[29] Rather than adopting new laws to address spyware, some comments suggested that the government could challenge these particular acts and practices as unfair or deceptive in violation of Section 5 of the FTC Act.[30]

Issues for Future Resolution

FTC staff agrees that a common understanding of what is meant by the term "spyware" would be extremely useful in discussing spyware, the problems that it causes, and possible solutions to these problems. In connection with the workshop, FTC staff offered a working definition of spyware, namely, "software that aids in gathering information about a person or organization without their knowledge and that may send such information to another entity without the consumer's consent, or that asserts control over a computer without the consumer's knowledge."[31] Panelists and commentators generally agreed that this definition provided a good starting point for discussing spyware and how it affects consumers.[32]

FTC staff believes that the workshop discussions and related information provided important insights concerning how to address the conceptual challenges associated with defining spyware. There appears to be broad agreement that spyware should be defined to include software installed without adequate consent from the user. It also appears that, because both monitoring software and non-monitoring software can cause harm to consumers, spyware should be defined to include software regardless of whether it performs a monitoring function. Finally, to avoid inadvertently including software that is benign or beneficial, the term "spyware" should be limited to software that causes some harm to consumers.

FTC staff emphasizes that fundamental issues remain to be resolved before a clear and definitive definition of spyware can emerge. Software distributors should obtain consent to installation, yet there appear to be substantial differences of opinion as to what distributors must do to obtain such consent. Moreover, as discussed in Part III below, software installed without consent can cause any wide variety of harms to consumers, but there appear to be substantial differences of opinion as to when software has caused the type and magnitude of harm to warrant being treated as spyware.[33] In FTC staff's view, these fundamental issues of consent and harm need to be resolved before any common definition of spyware can be developed.

Prevalence and Distribution of Spyware

Prevalence of Spyware

Workshop participants generally agreed that spyware is becoming more prevalent on the computers of U.S. consumers.[34] However, the limited empirical evidence submitted in connection with the workshop does not permit quantification of the extent to which spyware has been disseminated. Researchers attempting to quantify such distribution have used definitions of spyware that differed in whether they included adware and cookies.[35] FTC staff believes that if a consensus definition of spyware is developed, it would assist in assessing the prevalence of spyware and changes in its prevalence.[36]

General Methods of Distributing Spyware

Software distributors disseminate their products to consumers through many different channels. For example, original equipment manufacturers install some programs on computers before consumers purchase them. Users typically supplement these software programs with additional programs they obtain from software retailers or download from software distributors' websites on the Internet.

Spyware likewise may be distributed through these ordinary channels of software distribution. According to some commenters, spyware may be included with software that an original equipment manufacturer pre-installs on computers prior to purchase, or with programs that users purchase from software retailers.[37] It also may be "bundled" with other software applications that may be made available to users at no cost, such as P2P file-sharing software,[38] screen savers, and games.[39]

Participants described various other means by which spyware is distributed as well. Users may receive spyware embedded in files shared over P2P networks.[40] Spyware may be distributed through email, including as an attachment to an email message, a hyperlink in an email message, or even in the email communication itself if it is in HTML format (*i.e.*, the email's contents are displayed as if it were a web page).[41] Spyware may also be installed from a web page.[42] As detailed below, participants emphasized that some spyware programs, particularly programs installed from web pages, are distributed by means that exploit browser vulnerabilities or use deception to undermine the ability of consumers to decide whether to install software on their computers.

Distribution Methods That Exploit Browser Vulnerabilities

One mechanism that web pages can use to install software is a technology called ActiveX. ActiveX is a tool designed by Microsoft to add interactive features to web pages.[43] The ActiveX technology is built into Microsoft's Internet Explorer ("IE") browser. In turn, some web pages include code (called an ActiveX control) designed to interact with the ActiveX technology in the IE browser. This interaction may result in the installation of additional browser-operated software programs, such as the Google search toolbar. Spyware developers can also use the ActiveX technology to install their programs.

As explained by a panelist from Microsoft, usually before an ActiveX-based program installs, a Security Warning dialogue box displays, telling a user the name of the program and asking if the consumer wants to install it.[44] Unless the user clicks on the "Yes" button, the program should not install.[45] However, some users change their IE Security settings from Medium – the default setting – to Medium Low or Low. At these settings, no Security Warning Box is displayed, and the software is installed without notice.[46] In short, by lowering their Security settings, these users have made themselves particularly vulnerable to the hidden installation of spyware.

A tactic known as a "drive-by" download allows spyware to be installed even if the IE default security level is unchanged. This tactic looks for various security vulnerabilities in the IE browser that will allow software to be installed from a web page without displaying the ActiveX Security Warning box.[47] Drive-by spyware distributors insert code into web pages, and this code exploits various IE browser vulnerabilities to install software without a Security Warning box being displayed.[48] Because users never see the Security Warning box, they do not know that the web page is installing spyware.[49]

Even if the Security Warning dialogue box is displayed, spyware distributors may use other techniques to undermine or misuse the ActiveX warning process. For example, some spyware distributors bombard consumers with prompts requesting permission to install software until consumers finally click "Yes."[50] Others may insert misleading or confusing information in the "Do you want to install" dialogue box.[51] Consumers may click "Yes" to authorize the installation without really understanding the purported disclosure.

Distribution Methods That Use Deceptive Tactics

Participants also described various deceptive tactics that distributors may employ to install spyware. Some of these techniques mislead users about the identity of the entity requesting permission to install software. One such technique is the "pop-under exploit."[52] With this technique, for example, users visiting their favorite news website are presented with a Security Warning dialogue box asking if they want to install a software program. These users may click "Yes" because they believe that the request is from the operator of the news website. In fact, the person seeking permission may be the operator of a totally unrelated web page hiding underneath the news website's page.

Other distributors mislead consumers about the source of a program through the use of fake messages that have been formatted to mimic a message that their Windows operating system would generate.[53] These fake "operating system" messages typically ask for consent to install software to fix a purported operating system problem. In fact, the "message" is from an entity that is distributing spyware.

In still another deceptive download technique described by participants, distributors may display what appears to be a window asking whether users want to install software. The "window" gives users the choice of clicking on a "Yes/OK" button, a "No/Cancel" button, or an "X" to close the "window."[54] In fact, the "window" may simply be an image embedded in a web page; clicking anywhere in this image, including on the "No/Cancel" button, or on the "X," initiates installation of the spyware program.[55]

Prevalence of the Various Spyware Distribution Methods

No panelist pointed to any statistics or knew of any studies showing how often each distribution method described above is used. One anti-spyware company stated that, in its experience, bundling of spyware with other programs is the most common distribution method.[56] However, it is difficult to determine the frequency with which the various distribution methods are used without a common definition of the term "spyware." Moreover, even with a common definition, it is often not clear to consumers or sometimes even software experts how a specific spyware program was loaded onto a particular computer. FTC staff therefore believes that public or private entities with expertise in the software industry should conduct further research on the different methods of disseminating spyware to assist in developing effective responses to spyware.

Difficulties of Removing Spyware

Software programs can usually be deleted with relative ease by using the Add/Remove Programs feature that the Windows operating system provides.[57] In other cases, a program might provide its own uninstaller. Several participants noted that spyware programs, in contrast, often cannot be removed using the Add/Remove Programs function and do not provide their own uninstaller.[58]

Workshop participants also elaborated on various additional reasons why spyware can be difficult to remove. One stated reason is that spyware programs may install as many as 4,000 files and make up to 2,000 changes in the computer's Registry (the basic configuration file for most computers with a Windows-based operating system).[59] To delete the spyware program, many of these files would have to be removed, and the Registry changes reversed or deleted.[60] Editing or revising Registry files creates a great risk that users will accidentally remove the wrong file, alter the wrong setting, or otherwise render their operating system or individual programs inoperable.[61]

Spyware distributors may also deliberately employ tactics that make their programs dif.cult to remove. For example, many spyware programs constantly change the file names and folder locations they use, thereby evading detection and removal by anti-spyware products.[62] Spyware programs may also hide themselves by using well-known file names belonging to legitimate programs.[63] Further, because multiple spyware programs may be installed with a single click, even if users delete the spyware program they are aware of, other spyware programs may remain installed.[64]

Finally, several panelists explained that even if users delete a spyware program, it may return on its own. In some cases, spyware accomplishes this by leaving a "trickler" behind when a user deletes it. The trickler gradually re-downloads, or "trickles down," bits and pieces of the spyware whenever the user is online, until the spyware is complete and operational again.[65] Other spyware programs actively re-install themselves or their settings as quickly as someone deletes them. These programs have two programs in memory. When one program is deleted, the other program will re-load the deleted program and any deleted Registry settings.[66]

In short, given the general lack of any easy means of uninstalling and the use of tactics to resist removal, FTC staff concludes that most spyware is more difficult – often much more difficult – to remove from computers than other software. This exacerbates the adverse effects of spyware described below.

THE EFFECTS OF SPYWARE

FTC staff concludes that spyware can harm computer operation and performance, increase privacy and confidentiality risks, make computers less secure, and impose significant costs on businesses. Panelists and commenters presented no empirical data, however, that quantified the nature and extent of these harms or benefits.

Impact of Spyware on Computer Operation

Spyware programs often cause significant degradation in system performance. Significantly slowed computer performance is the number one spyware-related complaint that computer manufacturer Dell receives, accounting for more than a quarter of all spyware-related complaints as of April 2004.[67] Spyware can even cause computers to crash. Microsoft reported that 50% of its customers' computer crashes are traceable to spyware.[68] According to panelists, spyware may use so many system resources that users are no longer able to use their mouses, and their cursors freeze.[69]

Spyware causes computers to malfunction in part because of the large number of tasks, or operations, it commonly forces a computer to run. One panelist noted that spyware can account for as many as 600 to 800 operations running simultaneously on a user's computer, as contrasted with the normal number of perhaps 30 or 40 operations running.[70] These system degradation effects were described as cumulative over time, and increase as additional spyware programs are installed.[71]

Another adverse impact mentioned is that spyware can result in loss of Internet access.[72] The explanation given for this result is that some spyware inserts itself into the chain of connections by which a user's computer connects to the Internet to watch what is being transmitted over that connection. Subsequently, when the spyware is found and deleted, it leaves a gap in this chain, thereby preventing the consumer from reaching the Internet.[73] Participants also noted that removing spyware can also impose substantial costs on consumers and businesses.[74] In severe cases, if the spyware cannot be removed, the computer hard drive may have to be erased and reformatted. If so, all systems, programs, and files must be reloaded, a process that can take hours if not days.[75] If users have not backed up their data, this reformatting process can result in loss of valuable documents, such as tax returns or photos.[76]

One panelist stated that some users have even found that it is less expensive to buy an entirely new computer than to pay someone to clean up a spyware-infected one.[77] In other cases, users were reported to have canceled their broadband Internet accounts and returned to dial-up access, because they believed the faster broadband connection made them too much of a target for spyware.[78]

Browser Hijacking and Other Changes to Settings or Files

There was general agreement that spyware can assert control over the operation of computers in ways that substantially limit the ability of consumers to use their computers. For example, some spyware programs change users' browser settings, which is often referred to as "browser hijacking."[79] Spyware may change the web page displayed when the browser first opens, *i.e.,* the home page, and frustrate efforts to replace that home page with the user's original home page.[80] According to one panelist, this is a common subject for tech support calls.[81] Spyware may also insert links to its own websites into the user's "Bookmarks" or "Favorites" list. In some cases, these links may lead to adult content websites.[82]

One panelist from a search engine company explained how spyware programs can redirect users' search requests to a website that the spyware selects.[83] The alternative website may display search results consisting of advertising links or links to adult websites, and even masquerade as the search engine users thought they were using. One spyware program, for instance, intercepts search queries sent to Google, a popular search engine, and then displays its own search results. The search results appear to be from Google but contain links to pornographic websites that would not have appeared with an actual Google search.[84] Panelists also reported that spyware can take control over users' computers through the installation of programs known as "dialers." The dialer program disables the Internet access phone number designated by a user, and substitutes an international phone number. Instead of calling their Internet Service Provider ("ISP"), users' computers place calls to the international telephone number, resulting in large telephone bills – as much as $5,000 in some instances.[85] McAfee reported that it had detected 4.2 million dialers on its subscribers' computers during the period from August 2003 through March 2004.[86]

Privacy and Confidentiality Risks

Consumer Privacy

Participants identified various privacy risks associated with spyware that vary in both scope and severity. These risks include the theft of personal information, monitoring of communications, and tracking of an individual's online activity.[87] Several panelists observed that the most serious privacy risks arise when spyware installed on a computer includes a "keystroke logger."[88]

A keystroke logger captures all keystrokes that the user types on the computer keyboard, including passwords, personal information entered into an online registration form (*e.g.*, a mailing address or telephone number), financial information submitted as part of an online transaction, and the contents of emails or instant messages.[89] Although some panelists stated that, at present, spyware that includes a keystroke logger does not seem to be installed frequently, they agreed that it poses a risk of substantial injury, such as identity theft, when it does occur.[90] Panelists also stated that spyware may monitor and collect sensitive information, including financial or medical information, about consumers. Some panelists suggested that the privacy invasion from such monitoring may be mitigated if the information was compiled in an anonymous or aggregated form,[91] but other panelists disagreed.[92]

Confidential Business Information

Panelists noted that businesses also face the risk that spyware will be used to access their information. The installation of spyware on a company's computer system could expose trade secrets and other confidential business information. It also could put the company at risk of compromising customer data in its possession, such as sensitive financial records, and lead to a loss of consumer confidence in conducting transactions online.[93]

There is little hard data regarding the extent to which spyware has been used to obtain businesses' confidential or private information. Many companies apparently are aware of these risks and often have taken steps to protect themselves, which may have limited the instances of unauthorized access or their impact.[94] However, one panelist noted that as spyware becomes more sophisticated, businesses may face increased privacy risks.[95] To respond, companies may face increased costs in protecting confidential business information, including sensitive customer information.[96]

Security Risks and Similar Harms

Interference with Security Tools

Panelists reported that some spyware programs have prevented users from downloading their Windows security patches or updating their anti-virus or anti-spyware programs. For instance, spyware may misdirect access requests and thereby prevent users from reaching the websites of McAfee, Lavasoft, Pest Patrol and other anti-virus or anti-spyware companies.[97] According to one commenter, some spyware will turn off users' firewalls and anti-virus programs.[98]

Increased Risks of Unauthorized Access by Hackers

According to one panelist, spyware that includes a keystroke logger can create security risks.[99] Such software is designed to enable the person or entity who installed the keystroke logger to monitor remotely the activities and communications on a user's computer. If the keystroke logging program is poorly written, it could be hacked into by persons other than the person who installed it, which would allow these unknown hackers to remotely record all of the activity on that computer.

Another issue raised was that spyware could create security risks by allowing hackers to exploit the automatic update features found in many of these programs.[100] These features update either the software program itself or the ads that are made available for display. One panelist explained that if update mechanisms are poorly written, hackers could use them to gain access into computers, with hackers being particularly attracted to programs containing such mechanisms that have been installed on a large number of computers.[101]

Usurping Users' Computers

Participants explained various ways in which spyware distributors can take advantage of spyware installed on a computer to access and use that computer for their own purposes. For example, some spyware secretly "borrows" hard drive space on computers to store its own hidden files.[102] Users are unaware that they are hosting these data or program files, and they do not know what these files might do (*e.g.*, they could be a virus) or what they might contain (*e.g.*, they could contain child pornography or copyrighted materials).

Spyware programs also may usurp computers by installing themselves in the shared files directory of a computer's P2P file-sharing program, using an attractive file name to entice others on the P2P network to download the file.[103] This can lead to rapid redistribution of the spyware program.

Finally, some spyware programs give the distributor the capability to join together the computers on which it is installed into so-called "bot farms" and take remote control of these networks of "robot" computers. Participants explained that, without the knowledge of the owners of these computers, distributors may use these "bot farms" in denial-of-service attacks against targeted websites,[104] to serve advertisements on websites,[105] or to send out spam email.[106]

Security Impact on Businesses

According to participants, the security risks associated with spyware are generally the same for businesses as for consumers. Many larger corporations, however, may be more aware of the risks and have information technology staff to address them.[107] But, as one panelist noted, a company's information is often its most valuable asset, so it would be a potentially devastating breach of security if its information were accessed, deleted, or transmitted to an unauthorized or unknown entity.[108]

Other Costs of Spyware

Costs of Responding to Calls to Tech Support

As detailed below, ISPs, operating system manufacturers, and computer manufacturers reported that they incur substantial costs resolving spyware-related problems. Consumers usually do not know they have spyware.[109] As explained by one panelist, they just know that their Internet connection or computer is not operating like it should, or that it is doing something unexpected – like sending out emails by itself, or opening to the wrong home page or search page.[110]

To get help, consumers call the tech support centers at their ISP, their operating system manufacturer, or their PC manufacturer. Dell reported that spyware had become the number one category of calls to its tech support staff by late 2003.[111] Likewise, McAfee stated that spyware has been a larger technical support issue for it than viruses over the past year.[112] At both Dell and McAfee, spyware-related calls have accounted for as much as 10% to 12% of all tech support calls.[113]

Participants stated that responding to these calls imposes substantial costs on businesses, which may be passed on to consumers.[114] One reason given is that spyware-related tech support calls usually take longer than regular tech support calls.[115] Because consumers often do not know they have spyware, tech support staff must troubleshoot to identify the source of the problem. One panelist reported that a regular tech support call to an ISP lasts about six minutes; spyware related calls average 25 minutes, which increases the cost of the call by about $15. Because subscribers typically pay $20 to $40 a month for Internet access, the cost of such tech support calls can severely decrease the ISP's profit margin.[116]

Costs Resulting from Lost Sales

Panelists also noted that spyware may tarnish the reputation of many high-tech companies. Some subscribers reportedly incorrectly blame their ISP for computer problems caused by spyware and cancel their accounts. One panelist estimated ISP losses due to higher support costs and increased cancellations to be in the millions of dollars.[117] A similar concern raised was that some consumers would blame the manufacturer of their computers for the significantly decreased computer performance that spyware causes, thereby making them less likely to purchase another computer from that manufacturer.[118]

Finally, some companies commented that spyware has cost them business in a more direct fashion – that is, by diverting consumers from the e-commerce website they intended to visit to the website of a competing seller.[119] In other cases, when consumers are browsing through the website of one e-commerce seller, spyware generates pop-up ads, based on the tracking information as to which sites the consumer is visiting, that display coupons or discount offers for a competitor's products. For example, when a consumer is reading about a particular book at an online bookseller's website, spyware may display a pop-up ad from a competing bookseller, offering that same book at a discount. These commenters complained that these tactics have resulted in lost sales, thus creating a disincentive for them to incur the costs associated with attracting consumers to their websites.[120]

Potential Benefits of Spyware to Consumers or Competition

Panelists and commenters emphasized that users may receive benefits from some monitoring software installed on their computers. Monitoring software can allow parents to track computer use by their children. It also can allow tech support to perform remote diagnostic tests of computer systems, track inventory flows, and assist in inspecting computers for security protection.[121] However, users or owners of the computers involved typically have consented to the installation of such monitoring software, and so FTC staff believes that such software usually would not be treated as spyware. Accordingly, it seems that the benefits resulting from monitoring software are not properly attributable to spyware.

Panelists and commenters also asserted that consumers and competition may benefit from the dissemination of adware. Consumers often may receive other software for free if they are willing to accept an adware program.[122] Consumers also may receive offers targeted to their particular preferences and experiences or other attractive offers as a result of the ads.[123] As discussed above in Part II.A.2., there is substantial dispute as to when adware should be considered spyware, and, therefore, FTC staff concludes that it is unclear to what extent adware's benefits are attributable to spyware.

INDUSTRY RESPONSES TO SPYWARE CONCERNS

As discussed above, consumers often are unaware that spyware has been installed. If they do discover the spyware, they may not know what to do to remove it, or may be concerned that attempting to remove it may inadvertently harm their computers. Given the difficulties inherent in relying on self-help to address spyware, many panelists said that a combination of industry and government action is needed to protect consumers. It was stated that industry's actions should include technological solutions, industry best practices, and consumer education.[124]

Technological Solutions

Basic Security Protections

Many consumers and businesses employ firewalls to make their computers more secure.[125] Firewalls act as gatekeepers between computers and the Internet, and they may be either hardware or software. They close unneeded ports through which Internet communications can enter the computer, and block incoming Internet communications unless the consumer has specifically requested the communication. Some also filter or block outgoing Internet communications unless the user has initiated them.

Although firewalls are important for computer security, a panelist explained that they provide limited protection from spyware. Firewalls generally will not prevent spyware from being installed.[126] They are designed to block specific kinds of threats and look only at certain attributes of incoming transmissions (*i.e.*, packets), much like the U.S. Post Office looks only at the addresses on a letter, but does not look at, or attempt to evaluate, the letter's content.[127] However, firewalls do provide some increased protection from spyware because they may alert users if installed spyware attempts to send out information that it has collected. With this alert, users may take steps to uninstall or disable the spyware.

One panelist observed that consumers could protect themselves better against spyware by using browsers that, unlike IE, were "uncoupled" from, or less integrated into, the Windows operating system, such as Netscape, Mozilla, Firefox or Opera.[128] For similar reasons, some experts also have suggested that consumers may want to switch to using a different browser.[129] Other experts, however, have noted that switching to a different browser may limit the functionality of sites that require features specific to Internet Explorer.[130]

Anti-Spyware Software

ActiveX blockers were one category of anti-spyware programs identified at the workshop. As explained by a panelist, these programs attempt to prevent the installation of ActiveX-related spyware.[131] ActiveX blockers generally work by maintaining a list of the ActiveX numbers associated with known spyware programs.[132] When a website tries to use an ActiveX control to install spyware, the ActiveX blocker checks the number of that ActiveX control against its list. If the number is found, the ActiveX blocker prevents the installation of the spyware. If the spyware has already been installed, some ActiveX blockers also prevent the spyware from running.[133] Some ActiveX blockers are available for free to consumers.[134]

Spyware scanners form another category of anti-spyware programs. According to one panelist from a spyware scanner company, consumers can use scanner programs, including many free programs, to scan their hard drives for the presence of spyware. If spyware is found, scanner programs typically offer consumers the choice to disable it, delete it, or leave it alone.[135] Many of these scanner programs are signature-based, that is, the scanner program's software developer analyzes copies of known spyware programs to determine what they look like when installed on a computer.[136] From this analysis, the spyware scanner develops a "digital fingerprint" for each program, and each digital fingerprint is compared to the files on a computer's hard drive to identify matches.[137] Because the digital fingerprint is only developed after a spyware program is discovered and analyzed, there is a lag time between the distribution of a spyware program and the ability of anti-spyware programs to detect it.[138]

One criticism raised about spyware scanners is that some scanners may identify particular programs as "spyware" even though some users might disagree with that assessment if they had full information about the program.[139] Another panelist noted, however, that to address such concerns, spyware scanners typically do not automatically delete programs after identifying them as spyware.[140] Instead, spyware scanners usually give the consumers the choice to keep, disable, or delete the specific programs that have been identified as spyware. However, another panelist stated that only a few spyware scanners offer enough information to help users decide whether to delete a particular program.[141]

Most anti-spyware programs must be installed on the user's computer. However, a panelist at the workshop identified at least one spyware program scanner that can be accessed for free and run from the Internet rather than from the user's hard drive.[142]

In sum, FTC staff believes that consumers can protect themselves from spyware to some extent through the use of ActiveX blockers and spyware program scanners.[143] FTC staff, however, offers the caveat that such self-protection measures impose costs on consumers. As noted by several participants, the current environment requires consumers to understand and become experts in the installation and use of anti-spyware programs as well as anti-virus programs,[144] and operating system updates.[145] An additional challenge stems from the need to update self-protection mechanisms, including anti-spyware programs, on a regular basis. Consumers need to know that the one-time purchase or installation of a particular program or technology to protect their computers is not a sufficient defense, and that they will have to make a diligent effort to keep up-to-date their anti-virus programs, system updates, and anti-spyware programs.[146]

Possible Actions at the Network Level

Some ISPs have made various desktop anti-spyware tools – primarily spyware program scanners and removers – available to their subscribers. AOL and Earthlink have made these tools available to approximately 35 million subscribers worldwide.[147] AOL's anti-spyware tool will automatically scan its subscribers' computers for potentially unwanted programs, display a list of the programs, and ask the subscriber if they want to disable any of them. Consumers can later re-enable the program if they find that another program with which it was bundled will not run without it.[148]

Another possible means to counter spyware would be for ISPs to block it at the network level before the spyware reaches their subscribers' computers. Some panelists argued that such an effort would impose added burdens on the network. They also asserted that it would place ISPs in the position of regulating their subscribers' Internet use, including the decision whether to install particular software programs.[149] Another objection raised was that it could stifle innovation in the software industry if ISPs were to decide which software their subscribers can install or which websites they can visit.[150]

However, several panelists stated that blocking spyware at the network level might work in some circumstances.[151] Business organizations, in particular, might want to block spyware from being downloaded onto their networks, because of the potential for great harm. A panelist gave as an example a keystroke logger installed on the company computer of an accounts payable clerk, which creates a risk of wide-scale fraud.[152]

Changes to Windows XP Operating System

A panelist from Microsoft described several additional tools for reducing spyware problems to which consumers using Microsoft's Windows XP operating system have access as part of its Service Pack 2 ("SP2") update for the XP operating system. Because ActiveX downloads often are initiated when a computer user clicks on a pop-up window, SP2 includes a pop-up blocker. Consumers are able to view blocked pop-ups from a particular site if they wish to, and can choose whether to turn the blocker off entirely.[153]

Another SP2 feature prevents unsolicited, ActiveX-related software downloads. If an ActiveX control tries to download software, instead of displaying the Security Warning dialogue box that asks users if they want to install the software, a one-line message is displayed stating that the installation of software was blocked. Users can unblock the installation should they decide later that they actually need or want that software.[154] This particular change is intended to avoid interrupting the user's Internet experience and prevent the user from accidentally or hurriedly clicking "Yes" to an unwanted download. In addition, it is expected that this update will reduce incidences of children accidentally clicking "Yes" to the "do you want to install" question, because they will not even see the question.[155]

The panelist from Microsoft also explained the steps that his company has taken to redesign the Security Warning dialogue box itself. The space for the name of the software is smaller, so spyware developers cannot include lengthy fine print designed to confuse consumers. The dialogue box also includes a new option to allow users to check a "Never install software from this publisher" box to prevent the downloading of software from publishers that the user does not trust.[156]

Finally, the panelist noted that to aid technical support professionals in diagnosing and fixing computer problems, SP2 includes an Add-on Manager, which lists the ActiveX controls and other add-ons, such as Browser Helper Objects, that have been installed. The Add-on Manager allows tech support to disable, and thereby neutralize, those add-ons that are unknown, unwanted, or installed accidentally.[157]

Possible Future Changes to Browsers or Operating Systems

Another discussion topic at the FTC workshop was possible future technological changes to browsers or operating systems that could assist consumers in dealing with spyware. One panelist suggested the creation of a labeling system to identify the functions a particular program will execute. If users are considering installing a software program, their browsers would automatically compare the program's functions with the functions the users have said that they would allow and inform them of any differences.[158] This would permit users to set their own standards to determine which software programs – and functions – they are willing to accept.[159] They could also decide not to download anything that does not participate in a labeling scheme.[160] This labeling system could enhance consumers' ability to evaluate software that may be incompatible with their preferences, such as spyware, before it is installed.

Another possible technological change panelists discussed was an operating system that creates a separate compartment or "sandbox" for each software program and either confines that program to its own sandbox or establishes limits on what it can do outside its own sandbox.[161] This technique could prevent spyware tactics such as browser hijacking or co-opting a user's computer to send out spam.[162] A major difficulty of such an approach would be ensuring that the operating system could still be used effectively.[163] It would also require redesigning all Windows-based browsers, emailers, etc.[164] One panelist observed, however, that a sandbox does not have to provide complete protection and suggested that it is possible to look at certain relationships among files and design the beginnings of sandboxes.[165]

A similar idea panelists raised would be to design a "lockbox" for a Windows computer's basic computer configuration file (the Registry) that would require a program to obtain the computer owner's consent before making changes to this file. For example, because installing software makes changes to the Registry, users would receive an alert stating that a program wants to install and asking them to consent to the Registry changes and "unlock" the Registry file.[166] One difficulty with this approach is that most software programs routinely make a large number of changes to the Registry file, and thus consumers could be faced with frequent notices requiring them to click "Yes."[167] However, several panelists or commenters suggested that instead of designing a "lockbox" for all Registry changes, it may be possible to identify particularly critical Registry changes for which such alerts would be useful, such as a program's setting itself to run automatically when users start up their computers.[168]

FTC staff believes that many panelists presented interesting ideas on how future technologies might aid in addressing spyware. Our past experience with other technological areas demonstrates that market forces will provide high-tech industry with powerful incentives to develop technological solutions, although it is not clear exactly what that technology will be and when it will be available. FTC staff therefore believes that it will be important for policymakers to foster efforts and incentives to develop and deploy technological solutions.

Best Practices and Self-Regulation

Many panelists recognized that the private sector could play an important role in protecting consumers by developing a set of best practices for the software industry.[169] Developing a common industry definition of spyware was described as essential to this process.[170] Currently, each anti-spyware company has its own working definition of what is or is not spyware.[171] Panelists agreed that a possible starting point for defining spyware or creating industry best practices would be to identify those practices that everyone could agree were deceptive, harmful, or malevolent, similar to the efforts already being undertaken by the Consumer Software Working Group.[172] A panelist noted that private sector efforts might also focus on developing objective criteria for assessing software programs and a set of standards for their incorporation into best practices.[173]

A panelist with experience in industry self-regulation suggested that these industry discussions should involve a wide range of entities – operating system companies, security and anti-spyware technology firms, non-profit and consumer advocacy groups, and consumers.[174] In addition, this panelist suggested that the process of developing best practices should be transparent and open. Moreover, there was general agreement among panelists that the standards adopted themselves should be open, so that no one company can control their use.[175] Panelists noted that developing a set of industry best practices relating to spyware could be more complex than other self-regulatory efforts, because of the difficulty in identifying interested parties. In addition, there are many "bad actors" involved in distributing spyware who have no interest in developing or complying with industry best practices.[176] On the other hand, because best practices tend to distinguish the more responsible companies from less responsible ones, a panelist suggested that companies would have an incentive to adopt them.[177]

One panelist suggested that the optimal result might be a continuum of industry best practices. A minimum level of acceptable behavior could be established for all companies. Some companies could opt to do an even better job, with the expectation that they would be rewarded in the marketplace.[178] Another suggestion was that the private sector work to communicate any best practices to the public, and perhaps establish a seal or logo program, to help consumers readily determine whether a company is following best practices.[179]

Panelists agreed that disclosing information to consumers about these types of software programs was one of the most important best practice principles.[180] One panelist observed that, although some software programs currently provide a disclosure prior to installation, these disclosures often are insufficient because of their inconspicuous location or failure to provide enough information.[181] For instance, in the panelist's view, a disclosure buried in a lengthy end user license agreement (EULA) informing the user about bundled software may not be sufficient to provide clear and conspicuous disclosure. Another panelist proposed that, when providing notice, distributors of such software should clarify the relationship between the software program being installed and the effect of that program, for example, the display of pop-up advertising.[182]

Another proposal suggested by several participants was that best practices include a component to assist consumers in evaluating the merits of anti-spyware programs. Many different software programs are available that purport to identify spyware for removal, but some of these programs may themselves install spyware.[183] The private sector could establish certification procedures to test whether these programs performed as claimed, such as ICSA Labs currently does for anti-virus programs.[184] Such a certification program might be combined with a seal program.[185]

FTC staff believes that the development and implementation of industry best practices for spyware would be extremely useful.[186] Creating models for notice and consent to the installation of software would allow the high tech industry to use its expertise to identify various alternative means that distributors could use to effectively disclose information about software programs. Developing a common definition of spyware would help clarify what software anti-spyware programs should target and users should delete or block. Finally, given the difficulties that most consumers have in evaluating the relative merits of anti-spyware software, industry certification could prove helpful.

Consumer Education

Several panelists noted that the private sector can play an important role in educating consumers about spyware and anti-spyware tools.[187] One panelist described educating consumers about spyware as the greatest challenge that industry faces, in part because technology is evolving at a rate far faster than industry can educate consumers.[188] According to this panelist, there are [800] million computers in use worldwide, of which 50% do not have even basic protections against virus attacks, despite years of consumer education about viruses.[189] However, the other 50% – or 400 million computer users – have installed anti-virus protection, and industry can build on that base in addressing spyware.[190] Consumer education may be particularly useful with teens, because it is often the teens in a household who are engaging in the online activities that lead to installation of spyware.[191]

Participants also addressed what consumers need to learn about spyware. Consumers need to be able to make an informed decision prior to installation.[192] Panelists suggested that creating commonality in the program installation screens or the notice and consent part of the program installation process might help consumers know what to expect.[193] It might also provide them with the information needed to assess different types of software programs. Another panelist suggested that consumers should be taught how to determine whether or not to trust a website that wants to install a software program.[194]

Some industry participants have already initiated consumer education programs. For example, Dell reported that spyware-related calls to its tech support declined by about a third after it undertook consumer education efforts in early 2004. This suggests that industry-sponsored consumer education can be useful in combating spyware.[195] A panelist also mentioned the role corporations can play in training their employees, and the extensive consumer information provided by media news stories and online anti-spyware, security and privacy websites.[196]

FTC staff supports industry efforts to educate consumers about spyware, because consumer awareness is an important means of decreasing the dissemination of spyware and its associated problems. FTC staff believes that consumers would benefit if these efforts were expanded, especially in conjunction with similar governmental efforts to provide information to consumers about the risks related to spyware.

Assistance to Government Law Enforcement

As described above, computer manufacturers, operating system manufacturers, ISPs, and others in the high tech industry receive many calls from consumers to their tech support centers relating to spyware. As a result of these calls and their technical expertise, industry appears to have developed a substantial amount of knowledge relating to spyware, how it operates, and who distributes it. FTC staff believes it would be very beneficial if industry were to share such knowledge with criminal and civil law enforcement officials.

FTC staff also believes it would be useful if industry would provide direct assistance in government law enforcement efforts. For example, in *Seismic Entertainment*, a recent FTC spyware case discussed below, Microsoft filed an affidavit explaining the technical aspects of how the defendants exploited a security vulnerability in the Internet Explorer browser to distribute their software.

GOVERNMENT RESPONSES TO SPYWARE

In addition to private sector measures, government action also can play an important role in protecting consumers from the risks associated with spyware. Possible government action includes law enforcement, legislation, and consumer education.

Law Enforcement

One topic panelists discussed was the substantial law enforcement challenges posed by investigating and prosecuting acts and practices related to spyware – particularly the more pernicious programs.[197] First, given the surreptitious nature of spyware, it often is difficult to ascertain from whom, from where, and how spyware has been disseminated. Second, consumer complaints are less likely to lead directly to targets than in other law enforcement investigations, because consumers often do not know that spyware has caused the problems or, even if they do, they may not know the source of the spyware. Third, identifying the source of spyware is especially difficult when it has been installed by drive-by methods, given that consumers likely were not even aware that the spyware was being installed. Finally, once the distributor is identified, it may be located in a foreign jurisdiction, which can significantly complicate law enforcement efforts.

FTC Law Enforcement

Despite these challenges, panelists from FTC staff and Department of Justice staff stated that their current statutory authority was sufficient to prosecute spyware distributors. Section 5 of the FTC Act gives the agency the authority to challenge acts and practices in or affecting commerce that are "deceptive" or "unfair." The Commission will find that an act or practice is "unfair" if it causes or is likely to cause substantial injury to consumers, that injury is not outweighed by any countervailing benefits to consumers and competition, and consumers could not have reasonably avoided the injury.[198]

The Commission will find deception if there is a material representation, omission, or practice that is likely to mislead consumers acting reasonably in the circumstances, to their detriment.[199] For example, if a software distributor represented that spyware bundled with primary software would not affect the operation of a computer, this representation would be deceptive if the spyware used so much memory that it substantially slowed down the computer's performance or otherwise significantly impaired the computer's performance.[200]

It is also deceptive for a seller to tell a half-truth, *i.e.*, to fail to disclose information necessary to prevent some other statement from creating a misleading impression. So, if a software distributor expressly or impliedly represented that downloading its primary software would not cause a computer to crash, it might be deceptive to fail to disclose that accompanying spyware would substantially slow it down.[201]

Even assuming that the amount and type of information provided about the spyware is adequate, as explained above, software distributors often present it through fine print disclosures buried deep in a lengthy document. FTC law is clear, however, that disclosures must be clear and prominent if consumers are to be able to notice, read, and comprehend them.[202] The FTC has issued a guidance document providing sellers with information on how to present such information in an online environment.[203]

The FTC has substantial experience challenging unfair or deceptive acts and practices on the Internet as violating Section 5 of the FTC Act. Over the past decade, the Commission has brought over 300 law enforcement actions related to the Internet. In these cases, the FTC has obtained injunctive relief, and often, monetary relief. Specifically, the defendants in these cases have been ordered to pay more than $1 billion to redress harm to consumers.

Over the past decade, the FTC has brought 14 Internet-related cases challenging conduct that caused harms similar to those associated with spyware.[204] The Commission, for example, has challenged: (1) hijacking computer modems for use in placing unauthorized telephone calls; (2) hijacking web pages or "copy catting" website domain names to trap consumers and subject them to a barrage of pop-up ads; and (3) using information obtained from consumers who purchased an anti-spam product to send them spam.

Drawing on its experience in challenging unfair or deceptive acts and practices on the Internet, the Commission recently sued an alleged spyware distributor. The FTC filed a complaint in federal district court alleging that Seismic Entertainment Productions, Inc., SmartBot.Net, Inc., and Sanford Wallace engaged in unfair acts and practices in violation of Section 5 of the FTC Act. The defendants allegedly operated numerous websites and used a variety of tactics, including pop-up ads, to get consumers to visit these websites. Defendants then allegedly exploited a known vulnerability in the Internet Explorer web browser to download spyware to users' computers without the users' knowledge or authorization. According to the complaint, the spyware caused many different harms. Allegedly, it:

- modified the features of consumers' web browsers and hijacked their Internet searches;
- caused consumers to receive an incessant stream of pop-up ads;
- secretly installed a number of additional software programs, including programs that could monitor users' Internet activity and capture information they entered into online forms; and
- caused computers to malfunction, slow down, or even crash.

Furthermore, the complaint alleges that after the defendants had infected consumers' computers with spyware, they began to aggressively advertise to these same consumers purported "anti-spyware" programs called "Spy Deleter" or "Spy Wiper." The ads claimed that consumers must purchase these products to remove spyware from their computers. The defendants allegedly received a sizeable commission from the anti-spyware vendors based on the number of sales attributable to the ads displayed by the defendants. On October 21, 2004, the court granted a temporary injunction against the defendants. The defendants subsequently stipulated to a preliminary injunction.

Criminal Law Enforcement

In addition to the FTC's ability to bring Section 5 cases like *Seismic Entertainment*, the Department of Justice (DOJ) has statutory authority to prosecute distributors of software products, such as spyware, in cases where consumers' privacy or security is compromised. The Computer Fraud and Abuse Act of 1984, for example, prohibits the unauthorized acquisition of data from a protected computer that results in damage.[205]

The DOJ also has authority, under a variety of statutes that regulate communications, to pursue actions against entities that acquire information fraudulently, such as through the use of a keylogger program.[206] For example, the DOJ recently indicted an individual who installed a keylogger on a computer at his place of employment, and also prosecuted a defendant who had installed a keylogger on several public computers located in a Kinko's store.[207]

As explained above, federal officials believe that they have adequate authority under their existing criminal and civil statutes to take law enforcement action against those who disseminate spyware. Spyware is a serious and growing problem, and it has the potential to cause substantial harm to consumers and businesses. Notwithstanding the challenges posed by investigating acts and practices related to spyware, FTC staff believes that law enforcement officials should increase criminal and civil prosecution under existing laws of those who distribute spyware.

Legislation

Panelists and commenters disagreed about the need for spyware legislation. One panelist stated that in addition to industry self-regulation and law enforcement, legislation requiring the provision of specific information to consumers would provide another tool in the effort to protect consumers from some of the dangers associated with spyware.[208] On the other hand, DOJ and FTC staff panelists explained that their law enforcement efforts had not been stymied by a lack of federal legislation but rather by the inherent difficulties in investigating and prosecuting spyware cases. [209]

Proposed Federal Legislation

A number of legislative proposals focusing on spyware were introduced in the 108th Congress. The Securely Protect Yourself Against Cyber Trespass Act (SPY ACT), passed by the House of Representatives on October 5, 2004, would prohibit deceptive practices in connection with certain specified acts, such as browser hijacking, changing computer security settings, operating modem dialers or keystroke loggers, or using a consumer's computer to send spam email.[210] The SPY ACT also would require software programs that collect and transmit personally identifiable information to provide notice and obtain the consumer's consent. The Senate took no action on the SPY ACT during the 108th Congress. The bill was reintroduced in the 109th Congress in the House of Representatives on January 4, 2005, and referred to the Committee on Energy and Commerce.[211]

On October 7, 2004, the House also passed the Internet Spyware Prevention Act of 2004 (I-SPY Act), which would amend the Computer Fraud and Abuse Act of 1984. This bill would provide criminal sanctions for unauthorized installation and use of software on a protected computer: (i) in furtherance of another federal crime; (ii) to intentionally obtain or transmit personal information with the intent to defraud or injure a person or cause damage to a computer; or (iii) to intentionally impair the security protections of the protected computer.[212] The Senate took no action on the I-SPY Act during the 108th Congress.

The Senate Committee on Commerce, Science and Transportation reported out the Software Principles Yielding Better Levels of Consumer Knowledge (SPY BLOCK Act) on September 22, 2004. This bill would prohibit many of the same specified acts as the SPY ACT, when those acts are done knowingly and without authorization, and would require certain disclosures for software that collects and transmits information. In addition, it would prohibit surreptitious installation of software, misleading inducements to install software, and installation of software that cannot be uninstalled through reasonable means. The SPY BLOCK Act also would establish criminal penalties for unauthorized installation and use of software in furtherance of another federal crime or to intentionally impair the security protections of a protected computer.[213] The Senate took no action on the SPY BLOCK Act during the 108th Congress.

State Legislation

Various states have also proposed or passed spyware legislation. In March 2004, Utah passed the Spyware Control Act, which among other things, prohibits computer software from delivering advertisements to a computer under certain circumstances and requires that such software provide procedures for removal by the consumer.[214] The Utah legislation was preliminarily enjoined in June 2004 on grounds that it was likely to violate the Commerce Clause of the United States Constitution.[215] In October 2004, California enacted spyware legislation.[216] Several other states are considering legislation to address spyware.[217] Because of the global nature of the Internet, some support has been expressed for a federal, rather than a state-by-state, response to spyware.[218]

Consumer Education

The FTC, Department of Commerce, and US-CERT each have worked to inform and educate the general public about the issues related to spyware. In addition to hosting its workshop, the FTC has encouraged a public dialogue about the distribution, installation, and use of software programs such as spyware and adware. In conjunction with the announcement of its case against Seismic Entertainment on October 12, 2004, the FTC published a consumer education piece on spyware. The FTC is distributing this piece widely, including by posting it on the FTC's website.[219]

The FTC will continue to join with the private sector to encourage consumer education efforts by industry, as well as the development of best practices and robust self-regulation.[220] For example, on October 15, 2004, the FTC participated in a joint media event for the national press to publicize the FTC's consumer education efforts and launch the Consumer Spyware Initiative, undertaken jointly by Dell, Inc. and the Internet Education Foundation, which operates the website www.GetNetWise.org.

The Department of Commerce has focused its spyware education efforts on facilitating communication between the private sector and consumer and privacy advocacy groups. The Department, like other government agencies, seeks to balance the need to protect the privacy of consumers and businesses while preserving innovation and legitimate business practices.[221] US-CERT is charged with improving computer security preparedness and response to cyber attacks in the United States. It analyzes cyber threats and vulnerabilities, and then interacts with federal agencies, private industry, the research community, state and local governments, and others to disseminate this cyber security information to the general public.[222] US-CERT publishes both cyber security alerts and cyber security tips. This information is available in versions for home users and technical users.[223]

FTC staff concludes that government-sponsored consumer education programs are vital to informing consumers and small businesses about spyware, and the public would benefit if these efforts were increased.

International Cooperation

As discussed above, a number of panelists noted that many distributors of spyware appeared to be located abroad, which poses difficult law enforcement challenges. As federal and state law enforcement actions against spyware distributors increase, more distributors may move their operations off-shore. Improved cooperation and coordination between U.S. and foreign law enforcement officials would increase the ability of countries to take action against spyware distributors located outside of their national boundaries. The FTC testified before Congress in support of legislation that would enhance the Commission's ability to take action against foreign businesses whose acts and practices harm American consumers.[224] FTC staff is working and will continue to work with foreign governments to enhance the FTC's law enforcement and other efforts related to spyware.

CONCLUSION

The FTC workshop provided valuable insight into the nature of spyware, the problems it causes, and potential solutions for those problems. Addressing the problems associated with spyware will require a coordinated and sustained effort by the private sector and government officials. FTC staff is confident that the private sector and the government will undertake the measures necessary to protect consumers from the serious and growing problems associated with spyware.

APPENDIX A: WORKSHOP AGENDA

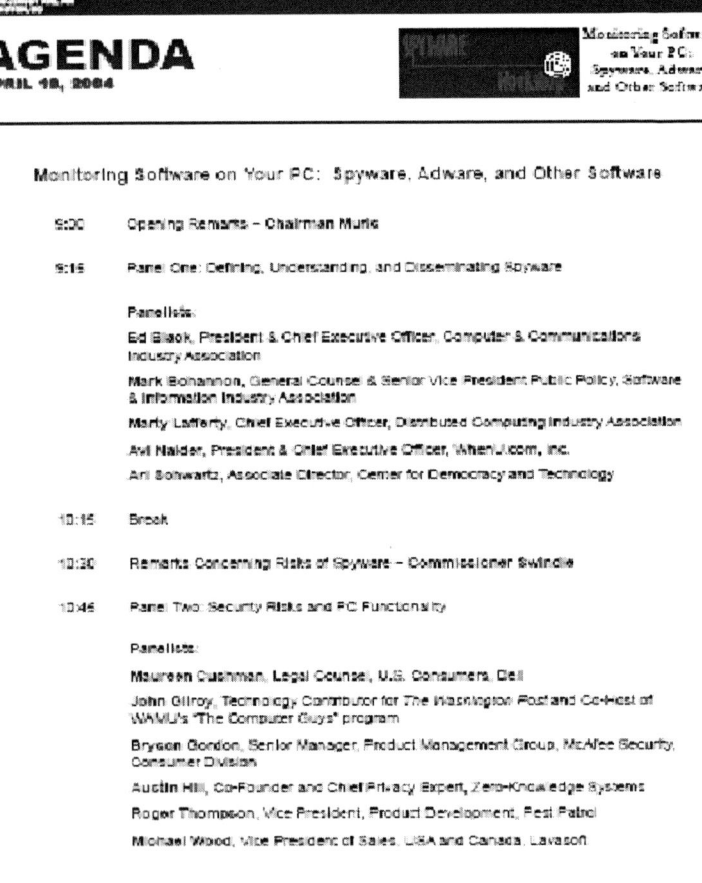

11:45   Panel Three: Privacy Risks

Panelists:

Ray Everett-Church, Chief Privacy Officer, TurnTide, Inc.

Evan Hendricks, Editor-Publisher, "Privacy Times"

Chris Jay Hoofnagle, Associate Director, Electronic Privacy Information Center

James H. Koenig, Esq., Chief Practice Co-Leader, Privacy Strategy and Compliance, PricewaterhouseCoopers, LLP

Ronald Plesser, Esq., Piper Rudnick LLP

12:45   Remarks Concerning Possible Responses to Spyware – Commissioner Thompson

1:00   Lunch

2:30   Panel Four: Industry Responses to Spyware – Industry Best Practices and Working with the Government

Panelists:

Brian Arbogast, Corporate Vice President, Identity, Mobile and Partner Services Group, MSN and Personal Services Division, Microsoft Corporation

J. Trevor Hughes, Executive Director, Network Advertising Initiative

Chris Kelly, Chief Privacy Officer and General Counsel, Spoke Software

Fran Maier, Executive Director & President, TRUSTe

Andrew McLaughlin, Senior Policy Counsel, Google

Jules Polonetsky, Vice President, Integrity Assurance, AmericaOnline, Inc.

John Schwarz, President and Chief Operating Officer, Symantec Corp.

3:30   Break

Monitoring Software on Your PC: Spyware, Adware, and Other Software

3:45 Panel Five: Technological Responses to Spyware

Panelists:

Steven Bellovin, AT&T Fellow with AT&T Labs-Research

Jeffrey Friedberg, Director of Windows Privacy, Microsoft

David Moll, President, WebRoot (maker of SpySweeper)

Wayne Porter, Co-Founder and Primary Editor, SpywareGuide.com (distributor of X-Cleaner)

Daniel Weitzner, Technology & Society Domain Leader, World Wide Web Consortium; Researcher at MIT

4:45 Panel Six: Government Responses to Spyware – Law Enforcement, Consumer Education, and Coordinating with Industry

Panelists:

Jennifer Baird, Legislative Counsel, Office of Rep. Mary Bono

Mark Eckenwiler, Deputy Chief, Computer Crime and Intellectual Property Section, Department of Justice

Mary Engle, Associate Director, Division of Advertising Practices, Federal Trade Commission

Elizabeth Prostic, Chief Privacy Officer, U.S. Department of Commerce

Matthew Sarrel, Technical Director, PC Magazine

Stephen Urquhart, State Representative, Utah House of Representatives

5:45 Closing Remarks – Howard Beales, Director, Bureau of Consumer Protection, Federal Trade Commission

APPENDIX B: SECURITY WARNING DISPLAYED

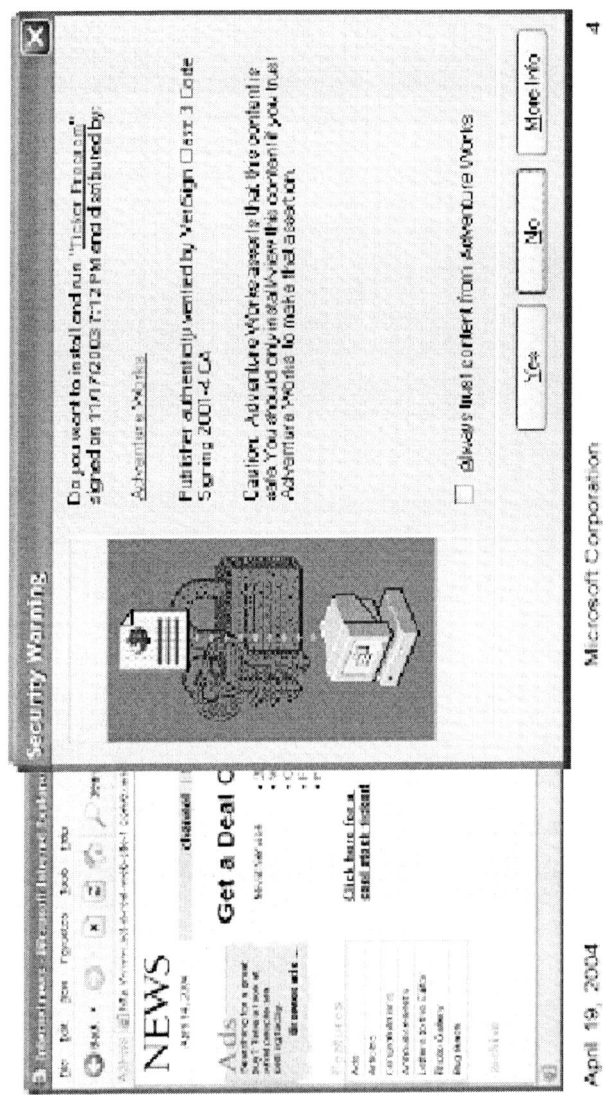

APPENDIX C: "CANCEL" MEANS "YES"

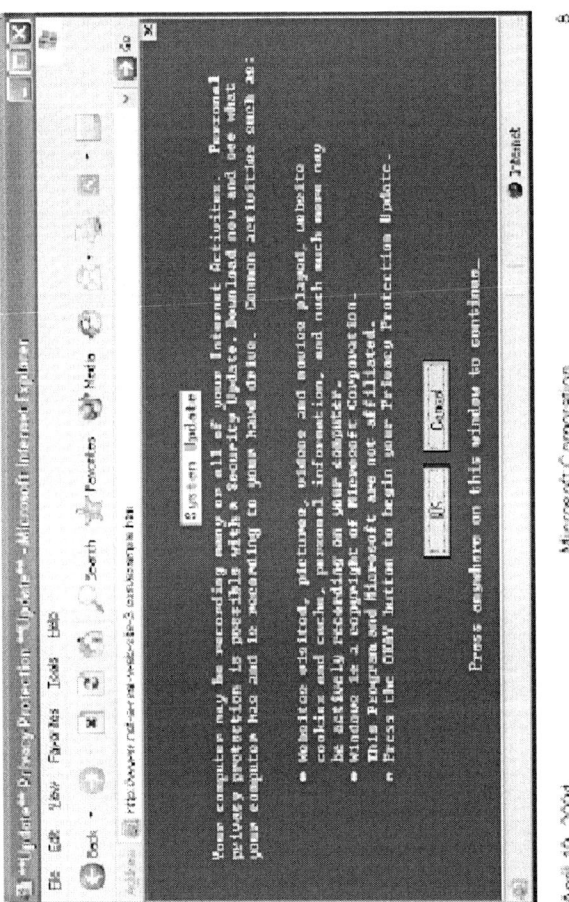

APPENDIX D: FAUX SECURITY ALERT

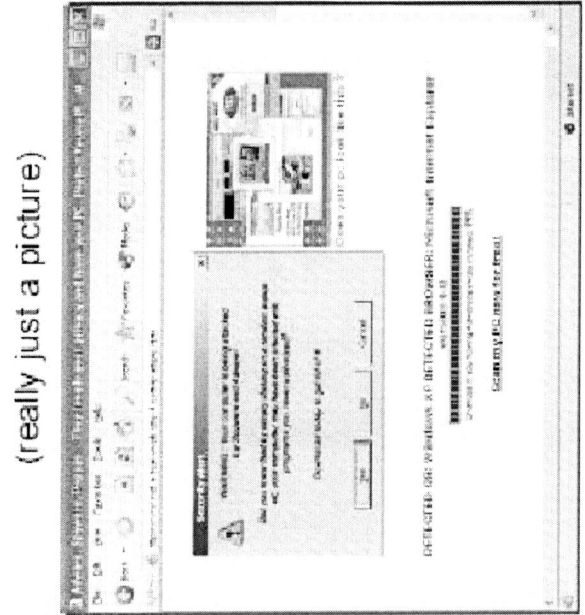

REFERENCES

[1] This report was prepared by FTC staff and does not necessarily reflect the views of the Commission nor of any individual Commissioner.

[2] The workshop agenda, transcript, panelist presentations, and public comments received by the Commission are available at: http://www.ftc.gov/bcp/workshops/spyware/index.htm.

[3] Beales, Workshop Transcript, pp. 11-13 (hereinafter Tr. 11-13).

[4] In connection with the workshop, the Commission received 768 public comments.

[5] Sharon Wienbar, *The Spyware Inferno*, C/Net News.com (Aug. 13, 2004), available at http://news.com.com/ The+spyware+ inferno/2010-1032_3-5307831.html.

[6] *Ibid.*
[7] Steve Gibson, Gibson Research Corporation, *OptOut*, available at http://www.grc.com/optout.htm.
[8] *See, e.g.,* PCWorld.com, *Business Strike[s] Back at Spyware* (Aug. 16, 2004) ("[S]pyware is said to encompass everything from marketing cookies, pop-ups and adware downloaded with peer-to-peer file-sharing programs to malicious Trojans and keystroke loggers designed to steal personal data."), available at http://www.pcworld.com; anti-spyware-software.net, *Definition of the term Spyware*, (July 12, 2004) ("If you ask 10 experts what the term Spyware describes[,] you will get 10 very different answers."), available at http://www.antispywaresoftware. net.
[9] *See generally* Panel 1 discussion, Tr. 15-62.
[10] Black, Tr. 19; Bohannon, Tr. 38.
[11] *See, e.g.,* Schwartz, Tr. 17; Lafferty, Tr. 21; Naider, Tr. 32-33. Some definitions of spyware, however, apparently do not require that the software be downloaded or installed without the consent of the user. *See, e.g.,* US-CERT Security Tips, *National Cyber Alert System: Recognizing and Avoiding Spyware* (Aug. 25, 2004) ("[Spyware] refers to a category of software that, when installed on your computer, may send you pop-up ads, redirect your browser to certain websites, or monitor the websites that you visit."), available at http://www.us-cert.gov/cas/tips/ST04-016.html; Webopedia Computer Dictionary, Spyware (Spyware is "[a]ny software that covertly gathers user information through the user's Internet connection, with or without his knowledge, usually for advertising purposes."), available at http://www.webopedia.com/TERMS/spyware.html. *See also* Hoofnagle, Tr. 133-34 (suggesting that notice and consent may not be sufficient because many highly invasive programs provide notice and consent).
[12] FTC staff has published *Dot Com Disclosures: Information About Online Advertising* (2000), available at http://www.ftc.gov/bcp/conline/pubs/buspubs/dotcom/index.html, to provide guidance to businesses about clearly and conspicuously disclosing information (including information about software to be installed) in an online context. As described *infra* in Section V.A.1, the failure to disclose information or to do so inadequately may be a violation of Section 5 of the FTC Act.

[13] *See, e.g.*, Everett-Church Tr. 139-40; Howes, Comment 59; Association of Shareware Professionals-2 (hereinafter "ASP"), Comment 352.
[14] *See, e.g.*, SEARCHCRM.com Definitions, Spyware ("Spyware is any technology that aids in gathering information about a person or organization without their knowledge."), available at http://searchcrm.techtarget. com; SpywareSurferBeware.com, *Spyware FAQs*, ("Spyware is the term given to applications or software that "spies" or sends information to the distributor of the spyware about your surfing habits, usually for marketing purposes."), available at http://spyware.surferbeware.com/spyware-faqs.htm; Spywareinfo.com, ("Spyware is software or hardware installed on a computer without the user's knowledge which gathers information about that user for later retrieval by whomever controls the spyware."), available at http://www.spywareinfo.com/ articles/ spyware.
[15] Howes, Comment 59 (describing the history of spyware).
[16] *See, e.g.*, Center for Democracy and Technology (hereinafter "CDT"), *Ghosts in Our Machines: Background and Policy Proposals on the 'Spyware' Problem* (November 2003), submitted as an attachment to Comment 10 (hereinafter "*Ghosts* attachment"); Sharon Wienbar, *The Spyware Inferno, supra* n. 4 ("Some in Congress call [spyware] 'cyber trespass'"); James L. Gattuso, *Locking the Door Against Internet Trespass: Are New Laws Needed?*, Heritage Foundation (Sept. 27, 2004) (spyware described as "trespassers on your PC"), available at http://www.heritage.org/Research/Regulation/wm575.cfm. *Cf.* Turner, Comment 184.
[17] For example, even if an individual software program might not significantly impair the operation of a user's computer, the cumulative effect of several similar programs could be debilitating. Hill, Tr. 110-111; ASP-2, Comment 352.
[18] A related issue is to what extent "cookies" are spyware. Cookies are text files (not software) that a web server places on a user's hard drive. The text files may contain a user's preferences or log-in information for a website. Whenever the user returns to that website, the cookie file is sent to the website so that the information in that file can be used to customize and facilitate the user's interaction with the website. Other cookies, known as "tracking cookies," record information about a user's interaction with multiple websites. For example, advertising networks may place tracking cookies on a user's

hard drive to record which other websites within the network a user visits. Cookies are usually placed without any notice to users, although most Internet browsers can be set to alert users when a cookie is about to be placed and give them the option of blocking the cookie. *See* FTC Statement, *Online Profiling: Benefits and Concerns* (before the Senate Committee on Commerce, Science and Transportation, June 13, 2000) available at http://www.ftc.gov/os/2000/06/onlineprofile.htm and *Online Profiling: A Report to Congress* (FTC June 2000) (discussing the role of tracking cookies in the development of online user profiles used to target advertising), available at http:// www.ftc.gov/os/2000/06/onlinepro.lingreportjune 2000.pdf.

[19] Naider, Tr. 32-33; Lafferty, Tr. 33-34. *See also* ASP, Comment 68 (discussing the history of adware).

[20] These non-targeted ads may be displayed via pop-up windows, but also by changing the user's home page or redirecting the user's search requests. *See* Section III.B, *infra* and McLaughlin, Tr. 164-66 and Presentation, Slide 6.

[21] Naider, Tr. 32; Lafferty, Tr. 34.

[22] Howes, Comment 59.

[23] *See, e.g.*, Electronic Privacy Information Center (hereinafter "EPIC"), Comment 199; Howes, Comment 59; ASP, Comment 68 and ASP-2, Comment 352; Turner, Comment 184.

[24] *See, e.g.*, Bohannon, Tr. 24; Plesser, Tr. 125; Consumer Software Working Group (hereinafter "CSWG"), Comment 197; ASP, Comment 68 at 1; AWS Convergence Technologies (hereinafter "AWS"), Comment 354.

[25] Bohannon, Tr. 25.

[26] *See* Spyware Control Act, Utah Code Ann. §13-39-101, *et seq.* (1953). In June 2004, the Utah statute was preliminarily enjoined on the grounds that it was likely to violate the Commerce Clause of the United States Constitution. *See WhenU.com, Inc. v. Utah*, Civ. Act. No. 040907578 (3d Judicial Dist. Ct. Utah June 22, 2004).

[27] Bohannon, Tr. 24-25. Bohannon described the Utah statute as defining spyware, in part, as "any software that monitors usage of the Internet and transmits information back" to a remote computer. *Id.* He also pointed out that this definition might apply to various benign Internet communications, including the underlying software for instant messaging, and that although the Utah law attempted to

address only pop-up advertising, he believes there is a serious risk that it also affects non-advertising pop-up windows.
[28] *See, e.g.*, Black, Tr. 19; Naider, Tr. 22-23; Bohannon, Tr. 24 and 52. *See also* Distributing Computing Industry Ass'n (hereinafter "DCIA"), Comment 32; AWS, Comment 354; Lavasoft, Comment 351 (stating that it bases its decision whether to include a program in its spyware detection tool on the program's behavior and the perceived intent of the developer).
[29] *See, e.g.*, Bohannon, Tr. 19; Lafferty, Tr. 20; Naider, Tr. 21. The Consumer Software Working Group (CSWG), an organization composed of high-technology companies, trade associations, and consumer groups, issued a report at the time of the workshop stating that there is a consensus that three types of software-related practices (hijacking, surreptitious surveillance, and inhibiting termination) are unfair or deceptive. *See* CSWG, Comment 197. Another comment would add to this list programs that, without notice, set themselves to run automatically at start-up. ASP, Comment 68.
[30] *See, e.g.*, CSWG, Comment 197.
[31] Federal Trade Commission, Public Workshop: Monitoring Software on Your PC: Spyware, Adware, and Other Software, 69 Fed. Reg. 8538 (Feb. 24, 2004). Available at: http://www.ftc.gov/os/2004/02/ 040217spywareworkshopfrn.pdf.
[32] *See, e.g.*, Naider, Tr. 22-23; Plesser, Tr. 124-25.
[33] *See, e.g.*, Lafferty, Tr. 20-21; Naider, Tr. 21-22; EPIC, Comment 199; Howes, Comment 59.
[34] *See, e.g.*, Cushman, Tr. 70-71; Gordon, Tr. 72-75 and Presentation, Slides 1-3; Thompson, Tr. 76; Wood, Tr. 76.
[35] For example, one recent study by Earthlink and Webroot counted both software programs and tracking cookies as spyware. *See Earthlink SpywareAudit Report* (Oct. 4, 2004), available at http://www.earthlink.net/spyaudit/ press (finding an average of 26 instances of spyware or adware on participants' computers). In contrast, another recent study counted software, but not cookies, as spyware. *See* America Online and National Cyber Security Alliance, *The AOL/NCSA Online Safety Study* (Oct. 2004), available at http://www.staysafeonline.info/ news/safety_study_v04.pdf (finding that 80% of study participants had spyware or adware on their computers).
[36] Participants focused primarily on spyware as it relates to computers with Microsoft Windows operating systems. Accordingly, most of the

information summarized in this report relates to Windows-based computers. It has been reported that spyware is less prevalent on computers with other operating systems, such as the Apple operating system. *See, e.g.*, John C. Dvorak, *Panic Over Spyware*, PC Magazine (Dec. 20, 2004), available at http://www.pcmag.com.

[37] *See, e.g.*, ASP, Comment 68.

[38] Schwartz, Tr. 45. One panelist cautioned, however, that the widespread use of P2P file-sharing programs and the large numbers of files shared over P2P file-sharing networks may have created the impression that P2P filesharing plays a larger role in disseminating spyware than it actually does. Black, Tr. 44. *See also* CDT, *Ghosts* attachment, Comment 10; Internet Privacy Conservation Council, Comment 29; Howes, Comment 59; EPIC, Comment 199.

[39] ASP, Comment 68.

[40] Thompson, Tr. 83-84; Gordon, Tr. 84-85.

[41] ASP, Comment 68.

[42] *See, e.g.*, Friedberg, Tr. 201-02; Howes, Comment 59.

[43] Friedberg, Tr. 202.

[44] For an example of this dialogue box, see Friedberg Presentation, Slide 4, attached hereto as Appendix B.

[45] Friedberg, Tr. 202-03.

[46] Friedberg, Tr. 207 and Presentation, Slide 10; Lavasoft, Comment 351 at 4. Certain programs may require the lower security settings in order to install, and users may simply forget to change the settings back to the Medium security level. Friedberg, Tr. 207.

[47] Friedberg, Tr. 207-08; ASP-2, Comment 352.

[48] Although spyware can be installed by any type of website, it is often installed by pornographic websites. Gordon, Tr. 107-08. Spyware is also frequently installed from sites attractive to children, such as game-related websites that offer game hints and "cheat codes" for the latest video or computer games. *Id.* at 108. (Cheat codes tell computer game players how to change a game to their advantage, for example, which keystroke sequence will gain them access to an endless supply of weapons.)

[49] Schwartz, Tr. 46; Black, Tr. 49; CDT, Comment 10; CSWG, Comment 197.

[50] Schwartz, Tr. 46; CSWG, Comment 197; Lavasoft, Comment 351.

[51] Friedberg, Tr. 203 and Presentation, Slide 6.

[52] Friedberg, Tr. 204 and Presentation, Slide 7.

[53] Often, these fake messages are formatted using a blue screen and simple text formatting or a grey pop-up window. The message may falsely claim that the spyware program is a "System Update" needed to protect one's privacy, or it may take the form of a "Security Alert" warning that one's computer is being attacked by spyware and claiming that the program is needed to get rid of the spyware. Friedberg, Presentation, Slides 8 and 9, attached hereto as Appendices C and D. Similarly, users may visit a website and be told that certain software is needed to view the site, when in fact the software is not necessary and is actually spyware. Schwartz, Tr. 45; ASP, Comment 68.

[54] Friedberg, Tr. 205 and Presentation, Slides 8 & 9, attached hereto as Appendices C and D.

[55] FTC staff notes that instead of clicking on the X, users should "close" such fake "windows" by closing the website that contains the image. In many cases, users can check whether the "pop-up window" is really an image by moving the mouse cursor to the upper left corner of the "window." If the "window" is an image, a toolbar will appear, with icons to save the image, print the image, etc.

[56] Schwartz, Tr. 45.

[57] In most Windows operating systems, the Add/Remove feature can be reached by clicking on Start, then on Control Panel, and then on Add/Remove. Use of this tool is the standard method on Windows machines for uninstalling programs from the computer.

[58] *See, e.g.*, CDT, *Ghosts* attachment, Comment 10.

[59] Thompson, Tr. 93; Wood, Tr. 103-05.

[60] In contrast, a virus may install itself in only a couple of directory locations and make just a few changes to the Registry file, making it fairly simple to remove once it has been detected. Thompson, Tr. 95.

[61] Gilroy, Tr. 104; Wood, Tr. 105.

[62] Thompson, Tr. 102; Wood, Tr. 103-04.

[63] Wood, Tr. 105.

[64] Thompson, Tr. 102-03. *See also* Naider, Tr. 57; Black, Tr. 58.

[65] Thompson, Tr. 103.

[66] Thompson, Tr. 91 and 102; Lavasoft, Comment 351 at 2. This self-defending technology – running multiple processes and when one goes down, the other activates – was borrowed from the virus arena. Gordon, Tr. 103.

[67] Cushman, Tr. 71.

[68] Arbogast, Tr. 161-62.

[69] Cushman, Tr. 71; Gilroy, Tr. 79-80.
[70] Wood, Tr. 112. When a software program is activated, it causes at least one, if not multiple, operations to start.
[71] Hill, Tr. 110-111; ASP-2, Comment 352.
[72] Cushman, Tr. 71; Gordon, Tr. 72.
[73] Thompson, Tr. 105. Several panelists stated that adware can cause functionality problems similar to those that spyware causes. Gordon, Tr. 75; Thompson, Tr. 110; Cushman, Tr. 110.
[74] One commenter stated that his charges for fixing a spyware-afflicted computer average $220, and have gone as high as $480. ASP-2, Comment 352 at 3. Spyware imposes costs on businesses because of the downtime required to repair computers that are not functioning properly. Gordon, Tr. 77; Wood, Tr. 80. Small companies lacking in-house computer staffs may also have to pay a professional to .x spyware-infected machines. Wood, Tr. 80.
[75] Hill, Tr. 109 (five days).
[76] Patten, Comment 274.
[77] Gilroy, Tr. 79.
[78] Hill, Tr. 95-96.
[79] Wood, Tr. 83.
[80] CSWG, Comment 197 at 2.
[81] Gilroy, Tr. 82-83.
[82] Turner, Comment 184.
[83] McLauglin, Tr. 164-66 and Presentation, Slide 6.
[84] McLauglin, Tr. 164 and Presentation, Slide 2. Another spyware program secretly substitutes its own search toolbar for Google's toolbar. McLauglin, Tr. 165 and Presentation, Slide 4.
[85] Gordon, Tr. 74; Lavasoft, Comment 351.
[86] Gordon, Tr. 74.
[87] Hoofnagle, Tr. 118-19; Plesser, Tr. 125.
[88] Everett-Church, Tr. 122; Gordon, Tr. 74.
[89] Everett-Church, Tr. 122.
[90] *Id.*; Gordon, Tr. 74.
[91] Lafferty, Tr. 34; Everett-Church, Tr. 120 (noting, however, that the use of deceptive tactics to gain installation would raise doubts about the truth of claims that a program only collects information in the aggregate).
[92] Hoofnagle, Tr. 117-18 (would also view collection of non-sensitive data as raising privacy concerns); *cf.* Hendricks, Tr. 119.
[93] Everett-Church, Tr. 123; Plesser, Tr. 124-25.

[94] Koenig, Tr. 126.
[95] *Id.*
[96] Hendricks, Tr. 128.
[97] Gordon, Tr. 82; Wood, Tr. 83. One method of doing this is to change the local Host file, which can be used to translate a domain name into the IP number assigned to its Web server that is actually used to .nd that site. If, for example, www.mcafee.com is deliberately mistranslated to the wrong IP number, users will not be able to reach McAfee's website.
[98] Turner, Comment 184. *See also* ASP-2, Comment 352 (Some spyware will detect and halt, or even damage, some anti-spyware programs).
[99] Porter, Tr. 248-49. This panelist described a similar situation in which a couple purchased remote monitoring software to enable them to track their children's online activities. However, the program had a security .aw that could easily be exploited to allow hackers to also remotely track their children's activities. Thus, by purchasing software to protect their children, they actually exposed them to additional risks. *Id.*
[100] Thompson, Tr. 89; Gordon, Tr. 89-90; CDT, Comment 10.
[101] Thompson, Tr. 84. Although none of the panelists were aware to date of hackers actually having been able to use update mechanisms to gain such unauthorized access, several expressed the view that it was only a matter of time before hackers succeeded. Thompson, Tr. 89; Gordon, Tr. 89-90.
[102] Gilroy, Tr. 87. In one instance, this panelist found a hidden three-gigabyte file (*i.e.*, 3,000,000,000 bytes) on a consumer's spyware-infected hard drive, and the origin and purpose of the file could not be determined. *Id. Cf.* CDT, Comment 10 (once installed, spyware may secretly download and install other applications).
[103] Thompson, Tr. 83-84; Lavasoft, Comment 351. Another panelist stated that if a consumer's computer does not have P2P file-sharing software, some spyware will install a file-sharing program on its own. Gordon, Tr. 85.
[104] Thompson Tr. 85-86. A denial-of-service (DoS) attack occurs when a network or server is deliberately overloaded with useless information to the point that it cannot handle legitimate traffic. For example, a DoS attack may direct so many requests for access to a website that no legitimate requests can get through, thereby "denying service" to other persons trying to access that website server. Such attacks

launched from multiple computers, as "bot farms" do, are known as distributed denial-of-service (DDoS) attacks.
[105] ASP, Comment 68.
[106] Gordon, Tr. 88. One panelist said that his ISP threatened to terminate his account because, unbeknownst to him, someone had breached the security of his computer and was using it to distribute spam. Hughes, Tr. 175; *see also* CSWG, Comment 197.
[107] Cushman, Tr. 77; Thompson, Tr. 77; Gordon, Tr. 92.
[108] Wood, Tr. 92. In fact, such a breach reportedly occurred when a keystroke logger deposited on a game developer's computer led to the game's source code being posted on the Internet and caused the company to forego a pre-Christmas launching of the new game. Moll, Tr. 248.
[109] The *AOL/NCSA Online Safety Study* (October 2004) conducted by America Online ("AOL") and the National Cyber Security Alliance ("NCSA") found that while 47% of study participants said they did not have spyware or adware on their computers, a scan of their computers showed that 80% of them did. Of those that did have spyware or adware on their computers, 89% were not aware of all of the programs found.
[110] Gordon, Tr. 72-73; Hill, Tr. 95-96; Sarrel, Tr. 283-84.
[111] Cushman, Tr. 70.
[112] Gordon, Tr. 72.
[113] Cushman, Tr. 70; Gordon, Tr. 73. According to McAfee, adware is the biggest single issue it is facing. From August 2003 through March 2004, McAfee's software detected just under 40 million adware programs on its customers' computers, with 11.4 million being detected in March 2004 alone, accounting for 86% of all unknown programs installed on these computers. Gordon, Tr. 73 and Presentation, Slides 2 and 3.
[114] *See, e.g.*, Hill, Tr. 95-96.
[115] Cushman, Tr. 71; Hill, Tr. 111.
[116] Hill, Tr. 95.
[117] Hill, Tr. 97.
[118] Cushman, Tr. 72. *Cf.* Plesser, Tr. 127; Hendricks, Tr. 128.
[119] Mondera, Comment 353; InterContinental Hotels Group, Comment 355.
[120] *Id.*
[121] Koenig, Tr. 147.
[122] Lafferty, Tr. 34.

[123] Everett-Church, Tr. 148; Naider, Tr. 32-33.
[124] Maier, Tr. 173; Hughes, Tr. 174-76; Schwartz, Tr. 182; McLaughlin, Tr. 191; Polonetsky, Tr. 186; Plesser, Tr. 131.
[125] Microsoft Windows XP comes with a basic firewall that must be turned on to begin operating. In the 2004 update for XP, the firewall is turned on by default.
[126] Bellovin, Tr. 214.
[127] Bellovin, Tr. 214.
[128] Hoofnagle, Tr. 130.
[129] In June 2004, the United States Computer Emergency Readiness Team ("US-CERT") issued an alert detailing various security vulnerabilities in Internet Explorer. The alert stated that "IE is integrated into Windows to such an extent that vulnerabilities in IE frequently provide an attacker significant access" to the Windows operating system. It also suggested that using a different browser would decrease these security risks. USCERT Vulnerability Note VU#713878 (.rst published June 9, 2004). US-CERT is a private-public partnership between the Department of Homeland Security and the CERT Coordination Center at Carnegie Mellon University.
[130] *See, e.g.*, Marty Sems, *Go, Go, Mozilla*, Smart Computing (Dec 2003), available at http://www. smartcomputing.com.
[131] Porter, Tr. 222. See Part II.B.3, *supra*, for an explanation of the ActiveX technology and how it works.
[132] Each ActiveX control or program code has a unique number, known as the Class ID, or CLSID. Porter, Tr. 222.
[133] *Id.*
[134] FTC staff notes that information on how to obtain free versions of ActiveX blockers, anti-spyware scanners and other anti-spyware tools can be found at non-commercial websites, such as https://netfiles.uiuc.edu/ehowes/ www/main.htm or www. spywareinfo.com, or at commercial websites, such as www.lavasoft.de, security.kolla. de, www.pestpatrol.com, www.spywareguide.com or www.webroot.com.
[135] Moll, Tr. 216. Disabling the spyware obviates the need to delete thousands of files or Registry entries associated with the spyware. Moll, Tr. 216.
[136] Moll, Tr. 216. The analysis may look at such items as Registry entries, the unique ID associated with an ActiveX control, specific files or directories, window titles, file size and hidden attributes, and

specific programming code. Porter, Tr. 216-17 and Presentation, Slide 2.
[137] Moll, Tr. 218.
[138] Moll, Tr. 221. To minimize this lag time, anti-spyware companies are attempting to develop a more behavior based detection mechanism that would allow them to identify certain computer actions as being associated with spyware, and then look for those actions in a program, as opposed to examining the filenames or file locations it uses. This would enable spyware programs to be detected without having to wait to analyze an actual copy of each program. Moll, Tr. 218, 221.
[139] Hughes, Tr. 175-176.
[140] Porter, Tr. 219. One panelist suggested that the use of spyware program scanners might have the side effect of encouraging best practices on the part of software distributors. If a distributor wants to avoid having its software disabled or removed, it will have to provide sufficient information at the time of installation to ensure that when the consumer is viewing the results of the subsequent spyware scan, he or she recalls the program and what it does. Polonetsky, Tr. 171.
[141] Moll, Tr. 216.
[142] Porter, Tr. 219. This program can be used on publicly accessible computers, such as those at public libraries, to detect spyware.
[143] Another category of software that does not directly address spyware but can be useful as a last resort in removing it are system restorers or reverters. These programs take "snapshots" of a consumer's computer system and settings at various points in time; some also take "snapshots" for all software programs and files installed on the computer. Friedberg, Tr. 243. Subsequently, if a new program installation adversely affects the computer, the consumer can "roll back" his system to a previous point in time before the new program was installed. One drawback, however, of "rolling back" a system is that this may also eliminate any files or programs installed or created in the interim. *Id.*
[144] Consumers seeking anti-spyware protection may benefit from the use of anti-virus software; the line between viruses and spyware is blurring, so spyware might be detected by an anti-virus program but not an anti-spyware program, and vice versa. Gordon, Tr. 72 and 84.
[145] Hill, Tr. 99 (noting that if it were equally difficult to drive a car, there would not be an oil crisis because no one would drive); Hoofnagle, Tr. 129-30; Howes, Comment 59.
[146] Schwartz, Tr. 172.

[147] Polonetsky, Tr. 169-170; Moll, Tr. 223-24, 226.
[148] Polonetsky, Tr. 169-170.
[149] Moll, Tr. 223; Bellovin, Tr. 224-25; Friedberg, Tr. 227.
[150] Bellovin, Tr. 224-25.
[151] Weitzner, Tr. 226; Moll, Tr. 227.
[152] Moll, Tr. 227-28 (speculating that spyware companies would stop targeting the credit card accounts of individual consumers, and instead, start targeting the bank that issued the credit card).
[153] Friedberg, Tr. 209.
[154] Friedberg, Tr. 209-10 (noting that web pages will usually indicate where they need a particular ActiveX control).
[155] *Id.*
[156] Friedberg, Tr. 211.
[157] Friedberg, Tr. 212.
[158] Weitzner, Tr. 234. A similar system for privacy policies, called P3P, or Platform for Privacy Preferences, automatically compares a consumer's privacy preferences with a website's privacy policy and alerts the consumer to any discrepancies. As a result, users do not have to actually read the individual privacy statements for each P3P-enabled website. Weitzner, Tr. 228-231.
[159] Developers of operating systems and browsers could be particularly useful in developing such a labeling system. Weitzner, Tr. 234. Similarly, industry could develop a community rating system, in which consumers relied on the ratings of a trusted source to decide whether to install a program. Arbogast, Tr. 191- 33
[160] Weitzner, Tr. 232-34 (noting that a labeling system could be valuable primarily for those spyware/adware programs that some consumers might want and others might not).
[161] Bellovin, Tr. 237.
[162] Friedberg, Tr. 238.
[163] Bellovin, Tr. 237.
[164] Bellovin, Tr. 237.
[165] Moll, Tr. 239-40.
[166] Panelists disagreed on the difficulty of drafting alert messages that would convey necessary information to users without confusing them. Moll, Tr. 243; Friedberg, Tr. 243; Hoofnagle, Tr. 130; ASP, Comment 68.
[167] Friedberg, Tr. 243. The result would be not only wasted time, but perhaps also to lull users into mechanically clicking "Yes" to a spyware request to install.

[168] Friedberg, Tr. 241-43; Hoofnagle, Tr. 130; ASP, Comment 68. *Cf.* Plesser, Tr. 132.
[169] Hughes, Tr. 175-76; Maier, Tr. 180; Schwartz, Tr. 181-82; Kelly, Tr. 167, 183, 197.
[170] Maier, Tr. 180; Schwartz, Tr. 181-82; Kelly, Tr. 183-84; Friedberg, Tr. 220-21. A common definitional structure for spyware would also assist companies trying to provide consumers with empowering anti-spyware tools, because companies are currently at risk for lawsuits when they identify a program as spyware. Weitzner, Tr. 219-220; Friedberg, Tr. 220-21.
[171] Friedberg, Tr. 221.
[172] Maier, Tr. 180; Arbogast, Tr. 191; Kelly, Tr. 197; Friedberg, Tr. 220; Kelly, Tr. 197.
[173] Friedberg, Tr. 220-21.
[174] Maier, Tr. 193-94. Maier also suggested that any such group should work with the FTC to get feedback, and may also want to conduct consumer research to determine what consumers think about spyware issues. *Id.*
[175] Maier, Tr. 193; Schwartz, Tr. 193; Kelly, Tr. 197.
[176] Hughes, Tr. 184; Polonetsky, Tr. 185.
[177] Maier, Tr. 173.
[178] Friedberg, Tr. 236-37. One possibility is that the "Always install software from X" option in the Windows Security Alert dialogue box could be adapted to allow consumers to choose to install software only from those following a set of best practices. Friedberg, Tr. 235.
[179] Schwartz, Tr. 181; Maier, Tr. 173; Friedberg, Tr. 235; AWS, Comment 354.
[180] Arbogast, Tr. 178; Maier, Tr. 180-81; Kelly, Tr. 183. One panelist stated that best practice guidelines might also need to define notice, consent, and the ability to uninstall differently depending on the type of program involved. Maier, Tr. 174, 180. For example, there might be different requirements, depending on whether the program to be installed was adware, a keylogger, or a parental control program. *Id.* In addition, several panelists suggested it might be better to establish privacy standards for all programs and not just spyware. Hoofnagle, Tr. 132-33 and EPIC, Comment 199 (stating that Digital Rights Management software is often privacy-invasive and resembles spyware); Hendricks at 136-37; Shaker, Comment 194.
[181] Everett-Church, Tr. 139-40. *See also* ASP-2, Comment 352.
[182] Everett-Church, Tr. 140, 144-45.

[183] Gilroy, Tr. 94; ASP-2, Comment 352.
[184] Moll, Tr. 244.
[185] Moll, Tr. 245; Bellovin, Tr. 246.
[186] FTC staff recognizes that bad actors would be unlikely to comply with best practice guidelines that industry develops. Law enforcement action likely would be necessary against such bad actors.
[187] Arbogast, Tr. 178; Kelly, Tr. 183. 188. Schwartz, Tr. 171-72, 181. Another panelist observed that consumers do not fully understand the risks to personal information associated with installing free programs bundled with spyware, and that they will not be receptive to consumer education efforts until they do have a better understanding of these risks. Sarrel, Tr.
[188] 281, 283. *See also* Cushman, Tr. 110 (need for consumer education about the ramifications of installing the software they are being offered).
[189] Schwartz, Tr. 171.
[190] Schwartz, Tr. 198.
[191] Maier, Tr. 194-95.
[192] Schwartz, Tr. 181; Arbogast, Tr. 197.
[193] Koenig, Tr. 134-35, 141-42; Plesser, Tr. 142. On the other hand, the install screens for a spyware program are identical to those for installing applications needed to view or play certain content. Consumers may be so accustomed to clicking "Yes" quickly to install the program needed to view the content they want, that they may click "Yes" automatically in response to a spyware installation request. Everett-Church, Tr. 139.
[194] Arbogast, Tr. 179.
[195] Cushman, Tr. 71.
[196] Sarrel, Tr. 282. This panelist also suggested that software retailers maintain kiosks, subsidized by software vendors, to provide information about spyware. Sarrel, Tr. 283.
[197] Engle, Tr. 258.
[198] Section 5(n) of the FTC Act, 15 U.S.C. § 45(n).
[199] Engle, Tr. 257-58. *See Federal Trade Commission Policy Statement on Deception, appended to Cliffdale Assocs.*, 103 F.T.C. 110, 174-83 (1984).
[200] Engle, Tr. 257-58.
[201] It is also deceptive for a seller to remain silent in circumstances that convey to consumers an implied but misleading message. *See Federal Trade Commission Policy Statement on Deception, appended to*

Cliffdale Assocs., 103 F.T.C. 110, 174-83 (1984). For instance, even if a software distributor says nothing at all about the fitness of bundled software, consumers may still take away from its silence that the software is reasonably .t for its intended purpose. If the spyware included in the bundle creates substantial security risks, such as exposing computers to hackers, the failure to inform consumers of such risks might be deceptive.

[202] Engle, Tr. 291-92.
[203] See *Dot Com Disclosures: Information about Online Advertising* (2000), available at http://www.ftc.gov/bcp/conline/pubs/buspubs/dotcom/index.html.
[204] See *In re Bonzi Software, Inc.*, FTC Dkt. No. C- 4126 (Oct. 6, 2004); *FTC v. BTV Industries, Inc.*, Civ. Act. No. CV-S-02-0437-LRH-PAL (D. Nev. Feb. 11, 2004); *FTC v. Baith*, Civ. Act. No. CV S-03-1306-LRH-RJJ (D. Nev. Feb. 11, 2004); *FTC v. D-Squared Solutions, LLC*, Civ. Act. No. AMD 03-CV310 (D. Md. Nov. 6, 2003); *FTC v. Alyon Technologies, Inc.*, Civ. Act. No. 1: 03-CV-1297 (N.D. Ga. May 15, 2003) *FTC v. Verity Int'l Ltd.*, Civ. Act. No. 00-Civ. 7422 (LAK) (S.D.N.Y. Nov. 21, 2002); *FTC v. NetSource One*, Civ. Act. No. 022-3077 (W.D. Ky. Nov. 2, 2002); *FTC v. John Zuccarini*, Civ. Act. No. 01-CV-4854 (E.D. Pa. May 24, 2002); *FTC v. RJB Telecom, Inc.*, Civ. Act. No. 00201-7 (Phx) (D. Az. Sept. 26, 2001); *FTC v. Hillary Sheinkin*, Civ. Act. No. 2-00-3636-18 (D.S.C. Aug. 29, 2001); *FTC v. Ty Anderson*, Civ. Act. No. C00-1843P *Federal Trade Commission* 35 (W.D. Wash. Aug. 29, 2001); *FTC v. Carlos Pereira d/b/a atariz.com*, Civ. Act. No. 99-1367-A (N.D. Va. Feb. 12, 2001) *FTC v. Audiotext Communications*, Civ. Act. No. Cv-97 0726 (DRH) (E.D.N.Y. Nov. 4, 1997); *In re Beylen Telecom, Ltd.*, 125 F.T.C. 276 (1998).
[205] 18 U.S.C § 1030(a).
[206] Eckenwiler, Tr. 260-61. *See also* Fraud and Related Activity in Connection with Access Devices, 18 U.S.C. § 1029, Title III of the Omnibus Crime Control and Safe Streets Act of 1968, 18 U.S.C. §§ 2510-22, and Electronic Communications Privacy Act, 18 U.S.C. §§ 2701-11.
[207] Eckenwiler, Tr. 261-62.
[208] Baird, Tr. 265-67.
[209] Eckenwiler, Tr. 259-62, 290-91; Engle, Tr. 258, 263, 291-92.
[210] H.R. 2929, 108th Cong. (2004). The bill, originally named Safeguards Against Privacy Invasions Act (SPI Act), was introduced by Rep. Mary Bono on July 25, 2003.

[211] H.R. 29, 109th Cong. (2005). The bill again was introduced by Rep. Mary Bono.
[212] H.R. 4661, 108th Cong. (2004), was introduced by Rep. Jim Goodlatte on June 23, 2004.
[213] S. 2145, 108th Cong. (2004), was introduced by Senators Conrad Burns, Ron Wyden and Barbara Boxer on February 27, 2004.
[214] Utah Code Ann. §13-39-101, *et seq.* (1953).
[215] *WhenU.com, Inc. v. Utah*, Civ. Act. No. 040907578 (3d Judicial Dist. Ct. Utah June 22, 2004).
[216] California Consumer Protection Against Computer Spyware Act, S.B. 1436, to be codified as Chapter 32 to Division 8 of the California Business and Professions Code.
[217] These states include: Iowa (S.F. 2200), Michigan (S.B. 1315 and S.B. 1316), New York (S.B. 7141), Pennsylvania (H.B. 2788), and Virginia (H.B. 1304).
[218] Urquhart, Tr. 275, 288.
[219] The FTC's consumer education brochure concerning spyware is available at http://www.ftc.gov/bcp/conline/ pubs/alerts/ spywarealrt.htm.
[220] Engle, Tr. 257.
[221] Prostic, Tr. 276-77.
[222] *See generally* http://www.us-cert.gov/aboutus.html.
[223] *See* http://www.us-cert.gov/cas/alerts/index.html and http://www. us-cert.gov/cas/techalerts/index.html. CERT also makes available articles aimed at home users that explain security-related issues in general. *See* http:// www.cert.org/homeusers.
[224] *Prepared Statement of The Federal Trade Commission Before the Subcommittee on Competition, Foreign Commerce, and Infrastructure of the Committee on Commerce, Science and Transportation, United States Senate* (June 11, 2003). The legislation, the International Consumer Protection Act, H.R. 3143, was reported out of the House Judiciary Committee during the last session of Congress, but the House took no action on the bill. The Senate Commerce Committee voted out a similar bill, S. 1234, which passed the Senate by unanimous consent.

INDEX

A

accounting, 39, 74
activities, vii, 1, 4, 7, 15, 16, 19, 22, 23, 24, 25, 34, 42, 52, 73
advertising, 3, 7, 10, 14, 15, 21, 22, 29, 33, 40, 51, 66, 67, 69
advocacy, 29, 51, 59
adware, vii, 1, 2, 3, 4, 8, 10, 17, 24, 33, 35, 45, 58, 66, 68, 69, 72, 74, 77, 78
age, 35, 36, 37, 40, 43
aid, 26, 49, 50
America Online, vii, 2, 4, 69, 74
anti-spyware, 4, 5, 6, 7, 13, 21, 26, 29, 31, 32, 37, 38, 42, 46, 47, 48, 50, 51, 52, 53, 56, 66, 73, 75, 76, 78
assessment, 47
attacker, 75
attacks, 43, 52, 59, 73
authority, 2, 13, 21, 25, 28, 54, 56

B

banks, 18, 25, 33, 77
BellSouth, 26
benefits, 39, 45, 54
best practices, 27, 45, 50, 51, 52, 59, 76, 78
Boxer, Barbara, 81

browser, vii, 1, 5, 6, 12, 13, 18, 20, 24, 35, 36, 40, 46, 49, 53, 55, 57, 66, 75
browsing, 3, 44
business, 10, 15, 27, 32, 41, 42, 44, 59

C

California, 2, 7, 8, 27, 58, 81
channels, 6, 35
children, 7, 45, 49, 70, 73
civil law, 53
commercial, 9, 75
communications channel, 6
community, 32, 59, 77
competition, 45, 54
competitor, 44
computers, vii, 2, 3, 4, 5, 6, 7, 11, 13, 15, 18, 20, 22, 24, 30, 31, 32, 35, 38, 39, 40, 42, 43, 44, 45, 47, 48, 50, 52, 55, 56, 69, 72, 74, 76, 80
confidentiality, 39
Congress, iv, v, 1, 2, 7, 8, 9, 10, 11, 12, 17, 19, 20, 57, 58, 59, 67, 68, 81
consent, 4, 6, 7, 9, 10, 14, 17, 18, 21, 23, 24, 30, 32, 33, 34, 37, 50, 52, 57, 66, 78, 81
Constitution, 58, 68
consumers, 3, 5, 6, 7, 9, 11, 27, 30, 31, 32, 33, 34, 35, 36, 37, 39, 40, 41, 43,

44, 45, 46, 47, 48, 49, 50, 51, 52, 53, 54, 55, 56, 57, 59, 60, 77, 78, 79
content, 7, 13, 15, 18, 21, 22, 24, 40, 46, 79
corporations, 4, 43, 53
costs, 6, 12, 39, 42, 43, 44, 47, 72
credit, vii, 1, 3, 77
crime, 16, 23, 57, 58
customers, 6, 39, 74

D

delivery, 17, 18
detection, 38, 69, 76
development, 2, 6, 52, 58, 68
disclosure, 32, 36, 51
domain, 55, 73

E

e-commerce, 44
education, 9, 10, 11, 30, 45, 52, 53, 54, 58, 59, 79, 81
Education, 30, 52, 58, 59
e-mail, vii, 1, 3, 9, 25, 35, 43, 57
employees, 6, 53
employment, 56
equipment, 15, 22, 31, 35
EU, see European Union, 32, 51
European Union (EU), 32, 51

F

family, 9
feedback, 78
financial institutions, 33
firewalls, 31, 42, 45, 46
firm, 2
firms, 51
foreign, 19, 25, 54, 59
foreign banks, 19, 25
free, 3, 5, 10, 33, 45, 46, 47, 75, 79
funding, 16

G

Google, 36, 40, 72
Government, 9, 29, 30, 31, 53, 54
groups, 29, 51, 59, 69

H

history, 15, 67, 68
House, 2, 6, 7, 8, 10, 11, 12, 16, 19, 20, 23, 26, 27, 28, 57, 81

I

ideas, 50
identity, 3, 6, 13, 17, 21, 24, 25, 28, 37, 41
incentives, 50, 51
industry, 2, 6, 7, 9, 10, 11, 29, 30, 32, 37, 45, 48, 50, 51, 52, 53, 57, 58, 59, 77, 79
Information, 11, 14, 21, 41, 66, 68, 80
information technology, 4, 43
Infrastructure, 81
innovation, 30, 48, 59
intelligence, 16, 18, 23
interest, 16, 51
Internet, vii, 1, 3, 5, 6, 7, 10, 11, 12, 13, 16, 17, 18, 19, 20, 23, 24, 25, 27, 28, 31, 32, 33, 35, 36, 39, 40, 43, 44, 46, 47, 48, 49, 53, 55, 56, 57, 58, 59, 66, 67, 68, 70, 74, 75
issues, 9, 29, 30, 32, 34, 58, 78, 81

J

jurisdiction, 54
justice, 15

K

keylogging, vii, 1, 3, 4, 13, 20, 25

L

language, 12, 14, 21
law enforcement, 15, 18, 22, 30, 31, 53, 54, 55, 56, 57, 59
laws, 2, 9, 10, 11, 15, 16, 19, 22, 25, 31, 34, 57
legal, iv, 2, 6, 7
legislation, 2, 4, 7, 9, 10, 11, 12, 17, 20, 30, 33, 54, 57, 58, 59, 81
local government, 59

M

Management, 78
market, 50
marketing, 3, 66, 67
measures, 11, 30, 47, 54, 60
media, 3, 7, 53, 59
memory, 38, 55
models, 52
monitoring, 6, 10, 15, 22, 27, 31, 34, 41, 45, 73

N

networks, 15, 18, 22, 24, 31, 35, 43, 48, 67, 68, 70, 73

O

oil, 76
operating system, 5, 31, 37, 38, 43, 46, 47, 48, 49, 51, 53, 69, 71, 75, 77
organization, 30, 34, 67, 69

P

parents, 7, 45
password, 3, 13, 21, 25
Pennsylvania, 81
performance, 5, 30, 32, 39, 44, 55

policies, v, 1, 25, 67, 77, 79
politics, 27
pop-up ads, 3, 4, 5, 6, 7, 10, 33, 44, 55, 56, 66
pop-up windows, 5, 68, 69
ports, 46
primary, 32, 54, 55
privacy, 2, 4, 11, 18, 24, 25, 29, 30, 31, 39, 41, 53, 56, 59, 71, 72, 77, 78
private sector, 6, 31, 50, 51, 52, 54, 58, 59, 60

R

ratings, 77
redistribution, 43
regulations, 10, 16, 18, 19, 22, 25, 33, 50, 67
relationship, 51
research, 37, 59, 78
responding, 44
responsibility, iv
retail, 17, 24
retrieval, 67
returns, 40, 67
risks, 6, 30, 31, 38, 39, 41, 42, 43, 48, 53, 54, 69, 73, 75, 78, 79, 80

S

safety, 26, 69
Sales, 44
saving, 5
Schwarzenegger, Arnold, 8
search, 4, 13, 20, 25, 36, 40, 43, 68, 72
security, 5, 6, 8, 13, 15, 18, 20, 21, 22, 24, 30, 31, 33, 36, 42, 43, 45, 46, 51, 53, 56, 57, 58, 59, 70, 73, 74, 75, 80, 81
self, 7, 9, 10, 11, 30, 45, 47, 51, 57, 59, 71
self-regulation, 9, 10, 11, 30, 51, 57, 59

Senate, 3, 8, 10, 11, 12, 19, 23, 25, 28, 57, 58, 68, 81
server, 67, 73
services, iv, 3, 14, 17, 18, 22, 24, 33, 43, 73
severity, 41
sites, 5, 44, 46, 70
software, vii, 1, 2, 3, 4, 5, 7, 8, 9, 10, 13, 14, 15, 17, 18, 19, 20, 21, 22, 23, 24, 25, 27, 29, 30, 31, 32, 33, 34, 35, 36, 37, 39, 42, 45, 46, 47, 48, 49, 50, 51, 52, 53, 54, 55, 56, 57, 58, 66, 67, 68, 69, 71, 72, 73, 74, 76, 78, 79, 80
staff, 6, 30, 33, 34, 35, 37, 38, 39, 43, 44, 45, 47, 50, 52, 53, 54, 57, 59, 60, 65, 66, 71, 75, 79
standards, 10, 31, 49, 51, 78
study, 4, 26, 69, 74
subscribers, 41, 44, 48
supply, 70
surveillance, 69
Survey, 26

T

technological advancement, 9
technological change, 49
technology, 4, 9, 10, 11, 13, 18, 21, 24, 36, 43, 47, 50, 51, 52, 67, 69, 71, 75
telephone, 40, 41, 55
threats, 4, 46, 59
trade, 6, 29, 41, 69
training, 53
transactions, 41
transparency, 3

U

United States (US), 58, 59, 66, 68, 75, 81

V

viruses, 43, 52, 76
vulnerability, 53, 55

W

web, 3, 31, 35, 36, 37, 40, 55, 56, 67, 77
web browser, 55, 56
web pages, 31, 35, 36, 55, 77
websites, 2, 7, 16, 33, 35, 40, 42, 43, 44, 48, 53, 55, 66, 67, 70, 75
work, 5, 46, 48, 51, 59, 78